Minnesota Music Teachers Association

The Profession
& the Community
1901 – 2000

Minnesota Music Teachers Association

*The Profession
& the Community
1901 – 2000*

Robert T. Laudon

Minnesota
Music
Teachers
Association

Cover: Richard Latterell, High School Young Artist Winner (1991) on Northrop Auditorium Stage with his teacher, Adelle Phillips, *photo by Mitchell Photography, Edina, Minnesota.*

Title page: Senior A Students at the 57th Annual State Honors Concert, 1 June 1991, Northrop Auditorium, University of Minnesota, *photo by Mitchell Photography, Edina, Minnesota.*

ISBN 0-9679777-0-3
First Edition 5 4 3 2 1
Produced by Stanton Publication Services, Inc., St. Paul, Minnesota

Library of Congress Catalog Card Number : 00 132867

Minnesota Music Teachers Association
11572 Landing Road
Eden Prairie, Minnesota 55347

http://www.mnmusicteachers.com
e-mail: mmta@sihope.com

Dedicated to Students—Past, Present and Future

Contents

Preface & Acknowledgements

As a new century arrives, the time has come to recognize Minnesota's glorious musical past. Many are taking stock. The Schubert Club, the Thursday Musical of the Twin Cities and the Matinee Musicale of Duluth have already published centennial histories. We await the opening later this year of the Minnesota Historical Society's major exhibition, *Sounds Good to Me, Music in Minnesota*. Within another few years we can expect the story of the Minnesota Orchestra (known as the Minneapolis Symphony in its early years), and the chronicle of the University of Minnesota's School of Music, each of them celebrating its one-hundredth birthday.

Within this volume, MMTA's centennial story is told from the early days as a pioneer champion of musical culture to its present status as one of the leading teachers' organizations of the country. For those who do not speak fluent Minnesotan, I should first explain that MMTA is pronounced quickly as a four-syllable word, much like "memorandum" but without any stressed syllable. It is as indigenous to the state as "ya sure" or "y'betcha."

In the last two decades of the twentieth century, MMTA developed in such complex ways that that period really demands a history of its own, preferably one made from the standpoint of the twenty-first century. As a consequence, the concluding chapter of this book, "A Work in Progress," is more a statement of the present state of the organization than a history.

Few organizations have had as many devoted volunteers carrying the message of music to thousands. A whole book could be made simply by listing their names. That would leave us little or no room for giving an account of the association's development. As the story unfolds, therefore, only one or two names must stand for the many individual workers who gave—and give—freely of their time and talents. Hundreds of names of important people must rest in the archives. A few are recognized here.

When I first was enticed into writing profiles of the MMTA presidents, I began to realize what well-educated and fascinating personalities sparkled in the past of the association. Their stories, miniature biographies, have been placed within the notes following the text. While they are fascinating to read in the present day and will serve a future historian who will write the history of music in Minnesota, they are extensive and might well be read *after* the history. An appended chronology, after the notes, will reveal the amazing number and quality of guest artists and scholars who have appeared at MMTA events.

Ethel Hascall started this project ten years ago. She compiled notebooks of special celebrations, collected memoirs of older members, inventoried the archives, read many drafts of the present text, chaired the Heritage Committee and alerted the members to the impending anniversary.

Mary Ann Hanley reviewed the voluminous file of *MMTA Newsletters* and prepared a synopsis showing the important changes in the association together with photocopies of the most significant pages. She also prepared a history of the certification process and its changes through the years. These files are so important that they will be placed in the association's archives to serve as guides to research.

Others prepared reports of the programs that they chaired for many years. I would particularly acknowledge Jean Hegland's help on the history of the theory program, and Clara Klatke's on the sight-reading program.

Several readers have made corrections and offered valuable suggestions, especially, Kevin Fitzpatrick, the editor and leader of the Lake Street Writers' Group and Dr. DonnaMae Gustafson of the Master of Liberal Studies Program of the University of Minnesota. Patricia Nortwen, current president of MMTA and Ethel Hascall joined Dr. Gustafson in the final editorial process.

Many from the research community helped in their usual efficient manner: the directors and staffs of the Research Library of the Minnesota Historical Society, Music Departments of both the St. Paul and Minneapolis Public Libraries, Archives of the University of Minnesota, Archives of Macalester College, Archives of the College of St. Catherine, and Special Collections of the Minneapolis Public Library. Particular mention should go to Patricia Maus, the archivist of the Northeast Minnesota Historical Center at Duluth.

These and many others have contributed to the photo and pictorial sources upon which I have drawn. Special mention should go to Bonnie Wilson, the Curator of Sound and Visual Collections of the Minnesota Historical Society. The secretary of the Evergreen Club, Daniel Tetzlaff, generously gave me access to the Old Log Book of the club which contains pictures and biographies of many musical leaders of Minneapolis. Penny Krosch of the University of Minnesota Archives provided important photos. Mr. Edward Kukla and the staff of the Minneapolis Collection of the Minneapolis Public Library provided still more. Francis Miller Aspnes allowed me long-term use of the mementos of her mother and aunt, Wilma and Ruth Anderson, leaders in MMTA during its early days. Mary Barbara [Ferguson] Spake, the daughter of Donald Ferguson, contributed a picture of her father, reminiscences and older books. Pictures of all MMTA presidents except Eugene Murdock have been recovered.

Historians of MMTA, past and present, cannot receive enough thanks for boxes and boxes which have been piled in my house for many months or even years—as Janna Rennich, the present historian, can testify. At least two short histories of MMTA have been consulted: the first, at the twenty-five year mark, by Jessica De Wolf and the second, a few years later, by Edwina Wainman. Among the early association historians, attention must go to John Hinderer who rescued many items from oblivion. Particular acknowledgement must be given to Russell Harris, who in his second term as president of MMTA (1983–1985), spearheaded the collection and organization of historical material.

Finally, I must acknowledge those people whose names should be here and whose contributions have not been listed because they have fallen victims to the failing memory of a senior citizen, an elder who must also take blame for whatever shortcomings still exist.

Robert T. Laudon
Minneapolis, Minnesota
February 2000

1

Building the Musical Gibraltar
of the Great Northwest

In the 1880s a remarkable group of musical leaders from other states and other countries chose Minnesota as their home. Some had searched the entire nation before making their choice of St. Paul, Minneapolis, or Duluth. The immigrants were attracted by economic prosperity, natural wonders, and the vigor of the rapidly-growing populace. Minnesota promised a bright future as the Gateway to the Great Northwest. The newcomers saw no reason why they could not develop a Musical Gibraltar of the Great Northwest to match the economic one.[1]

They found, on arrival, singing schools supervised by Yankee professors, choruses maintained by churches and ethnic groups, bands organized by military and private leaders, and a strong musical training program established by the Order of St. Joseph of Carondelet. They discovered women of the state, stalwarts of the club movement, eager to study musical art.

Bustling with enthusiasm and full of idealism, this group of musicians wanted to promote concert music. They also wanted to teach—not just as a means of sustenance but as an opportunity to pass on the musical heritage they cherished. However great discrepancies were apparent. Some instruction was world-class, some quite primitive. If they were to establish high standards throughout the state, Minnesotans needed to band together with concerted action. They needed to form a music teachers association.

Such an organization existed on a national level: MTNA, the Music Teachers National Association. A group of Ohio teachers had founded MTNA in 1876. It had by the 1880s spread throughout the Midwest. Each year, in various cities of the nation, musicians of MTNA gathered at conventions to share performances, problems, and teaching methods as they worked toward higher standards.

Minnesota first sent a representative, William H. Leib,[2] to the Chicago MTNA Convention in 1882. There he was appointed Vice-President for

William H. Leib

Minnesota. In this capacity, he was expected to bring the knowledge of the national leaders back to Minnesota and to promote the establishment of a state music teachers association. The state organization in turn would then elect or appoint a vice-president for each county who would in similar fashion bring ideas to all localities. In short, MTNA proposed a great chain extending from top national musicians and teachers through a system of vice-presidents down to each local teacher. The fervent hope was that professional standards would then become widespread throughout the nation and the benefits of first-class music instruction would be available in every hamlet.

Leib served in this vice-presidential post until 1885 at which point he left the state and others took on his responsibilities. Reports of national activities continued to be transmitted back to Minnesota but no state association was formed. Then in 1887, Vice-President for Minnesota, Charles Morse,[3] went to Indianapolis and told the national convention: "We plan to meet the first week in October . . . and when the State Association is working . . . a decided improvement in professional standards and a consequent uplifting of public taste will result."[4]

In keeping with this plan, the Superintendant of Music in the Public Schools of Minneapolis, O. E. McFadon, invited Minnesota music teachers to meet in St. Paul at Ford's Music Hall on Wednesday, 19 October 1887. Because the meeting coincided with a concert in Minneapolis, attendance was slim. Despite this difficulty, the group elected state officers and vice-presidents for a few counties of Minnesota. Willard Patton,[5] dean of Minnesota composers and prime mover in the establishment of MMTA, became president of the fledgling association which would "further the spirit of good fellowship among the teachers of the *divine art.*"[6]

This group met again in Dyer Music Hall, Minneapolis, 30 October 1887. After performances by ten of their members, they adopted a constitution.

Willard Patton

Thirty members were enrolled. Patton considered that a good start. About the same number had launched the Ohio and Indiana Music Teachers Associations.[7]

Though the moment seemed propitious, the state organization, MMTA, found it difficult to keep interest alive. Two years after its inception, several Minnesota members formed the opinion that if a national meeting were held in Minnesota, it would boost the faltering state organization. Consequently in Philadelphia in 1889, the Vice-President for Minnesota, Walter Petzet,[8] made the plea and received approval for a Minneapolis national convention with the following state officers making local arrangements.[9]

President	Willard Patton	Minneapolis
Secretary	William A. Wheaton	St. Paul
Executive Committee	Carl V. Lachmund	Minneapolis
	S. A. Baldwin	St. Paul
	Gustavus Johnson	Minneapolis

As plans for the convention began to take shape and the Minnesotans began to solicit attendance, another more prestigious event took precedence: the Tenth Republican National Convention in Minneapolis, the first to be held west of Chicago. Faced with this crush of events—some 100,000 to 125,000 visitors were expected—and with the persistent difficulty of recruiting members, MMTA cancelled its plans for a 1892 convention in Minneapolis and the national organization moved it with some difficulty to Cleveland.[10]

After this setback, the Minnesota association became quiescent for the next nine years. Within this period, certain members continued to attend national meetings where they presented the high ideals of the pioneer Minnesotans. Mrs. K. M. Strong, instructor at Albert Lea College, for instance, championed in 1900 the idea that the well-prepared teacher would bring the art of music to its true dignity as opposed to the amateur teacher who could do actual harm.[11] So great was the interest of Minnesotans that each year 8 to 15 persons attended the national conventions. A few even served on national committees: Clarance Marshall on the committee for methods and results concerning music in the schools and Charles H. Congdon on the auditing committee. Unfortunately this interest on the part of leaders was not matched by action within the state and the organization of a MMTA still remained a dream.

Such a story of demise and rebirth was common in the early days of music teachers organizations. The national group in that period had roughly twenty-five state vice-presidents but usually only about a dozen fully-operative state units. Minnesota mirrored the experience of other states caught between national activity and state lethargy.

It was in 1901 that the state finally formed its own association, an organization destined to last for a century and foster the "divine art"—as it was frequently called—in Minnesota. Immediate help came from the Professional League, a social organization of musicians formed in St. Paul around 1898 by Eugene C. Murdock,[12] pianist and composer, one of many New Englanders transplanted to Minnesota.

The League and its president, Murdock, issued a call for a meeting on 27 June 1901 "to organize a State Music Teachers Association." On that day, they produced, within four hours, a simple constitution paralleling the national one.

I. **Name:** *The name of this organization shall be "The Minnesota State Music Teachers' Association."*

II. **Object:** *To promote the true culture of music by interchange of ideas, advance the musical art and foster professional fraternity.*

III. **Membership:** *(a) To become an active member one must have been a resident of the state one year, and must be a professional teacher of voice culture, pianoforte, organ, or any one of the legitimate instruments of the orchestra, or any subject pertaining to the theory of music. (b) Active members shall pay an annual fee of $2.*

IV. **Officers:** *The officers shall be: A President, First Vice-President, Secretary-Treasurer, Auditor and Program Committee of three. These officers shall be elected by ballot and act as an Executive Board. In addition to these elective officers, the President shall have the power to appoint a Vice-President for each county, and the Executive Board shall appoint a Local Executive Committee.*

V. **Meetings:** *This Association shall meet annually, the time and place of meeting to be determined by the Association.*

The group elected Clarance Marshall[13] president, decided to meet in St Paul the next year, thanked the ladies of the League for their "kindly hospitality," and adjourned in time "for delegates to take the evening trains, if they so desire." A gratifying conclusion to so many years of hope and disappointment![14]

They had set before the state a goal that was to guide the organization throughout its lifetime: "To promote the true culture of music" and not "mere dexterity in the use of voice or fingers."[15] For this generation—often termed the "cultured generation"—that meant the profound works, particularly those by the composers of the German-speaking nations: Bach, Beethoven, Mozart, Brahms, Wagner, Schubert, and Schumann. These were to be studied and performed with professional standards.

In their choice of Marshall, the group found the best leader in Minnesota. He had studied with Professor John Knowles Paine of Harvard University and the noted Boston conductor, Carl Zerrahn. He possessed sound musicianship,

Clarance A. Marshall

and equally important to MMTA in its formative years, he had proven business acumen. For ten years he had directed the Northwestern Conservatory in
Minneapolis and had drawn the community into his conservatory operation
by including in his Board of Visitors a distinguished group of citizens: the presidents of the State University, Carleton College, the Thursday Musicale, the
Schubert Club and various leaders in business. With such backing, he made his
conservatory in essence the Music Department of the State University where
university students could study music and conservatory students could through
reciprocity take university courses.

After the first organizational meeting of 1901, a large convention was
planned for 1902. It was preceded by a flurry of activity. Five thousand cir-
culars and thousands of program agendas went out to all parts of Minnesota.
A guarantee of $300 from St. Paul musicians and $200 from advertising covered these initial expenses. Consequently, when President Marshall took the
podium 19 and 20 May 1902 in the Central Presbyterian Church of St. Paul,
he could look to an MMTA that had grown from 47 charter members to
133. With pride he could sail into his "address"—one did not give "talks" in
those days but something grander—with unbridled optimism.

> We feel that this first annual meeting, ambitious though it may be
> in some respects, will be but a small beginning toward longer,
> better, grander meetings in the future; a future which will see

> double the number of sessions, double the number of members,
> double the enthusiasm and double the artistic benefit to the mu-
> sical development of our state.[16]

As he proclaimed that "the advance of Minnesota in matters musical has kept pace with the wonderful development of her farms, cities and industries," he thought of the conservatories, concerts, music clubs, and choral societies already established. He could dream but scarcely conceive that within a year, the state would also boast a symphony orchestra and a university department of music. Truly the state was on the move!

As the main order of business MMTA first considered how to improve music education. Caroline V. Smith reported that public school teachers were not meeting the professional mark either in general subjects or in music. Among 11,232 teachers in Minnesota, only 7% held college diplomas, only 32% had normal school degrees, 32% had high school degrees, and 39% had no degree. About 78% of the teachers had little or no training in music. A deplorable situation! And it extended to the state university! Harlow Stearns Gale, university teacher of psychology and member of a musical family, thundered: Music at the university was like the "snakes in Ireland, there aren't any!" Oh yes, several organizations for "war and fun" existed—the ROTC band for "war," the glee and mandolin clubs for "fun."[17]

MMTA, properly shocked, voted resolutions requesting a greater role for the divine art and sent them to the Board of Supervisors of the Public Schools and the Board of Regents of the University of Minnesota. Remedies for the public schools were slow in coming but the university heeded the call of MMTA and started a department of music the next year.

During this first convention, members were treated to four concerts by local artists after which a gala concert by the Kneisel String Quartet, the most famous quartet in America, capped the festivities for 1902.[18]

Quartet in E-Flat Major, Op. 74 ("The Harp")	Beethoven
"Lento" for Violoncello	Chopin
Andante for Quartet, Op.11	Tschaikowsky
Prestissimo from Quartet, Op. 17	Sgambati
Variations & Finale from D-Minor Quartet ("Death and the Maiden")	Schubert

This collection of favorite pieces was designed to appeal to the general public, which was admitted for a fee under the guise of associate members—a device for swelling the coffers of MMTA while advancing the cause of fine music—and incidentally enabling the association also to pay the Kneisel group $350.

A 51-page *Annual Report,* printing all the various actions and addresses together with the programs of its five concerts, followed the convention and made the group's achievements available to those unable to attend. This glorious beginning had substance, panache, and good fellowship—all of the items that seemed to foretell good results for the "great masses of the music-loving people" as the representative of St. Paul's mayor said in his welcome. The tone was set for the conventions of the first decade.

Survival, the major concern of the young organization, remained the focus of these early years. Membership varied considerably from year to year—generally within the range of 120 to 170. The musicians of 1901–1911 re-

---

Concert by State Talent
Wednesday, June 7th, 1905
First Congregational Church, Winona

Organ	Concert Overture	Alfred Hollins
	Gordon Graham, Winona	
Vocal	a. "With joy the impatient husbandman"	Haydn
	(The Seasons, Spring)	
	b. Marie	Franz
	Myron M. Blackman, Winona	
	Marc D. Lombard, At the Piano	
Piano	"Man lebt nur einmal" (Valse caprice)	Strauss-Tausig
	Miss Ella Richards, St. Paul	
Violin	a. Adagio religioso (D-minor Concerto)	Vieuxtemps
	b. Polonaise (ms.)	Alvin Kranich
	Maximilian Dick, St. Paul	
Vocal	a. Creation's Hymn	Beethoven
	b. Autumn Gale	Grieg
	Mrs. Jane Huntington Yale, St. Paul	
Organ	Pastorale Sonata	Rheinberger
	1. Pastorale	
	2. Intermezzo	
	3. Fugue	
	Gottfried H. Federlein, Minneapolis	
Cello	Kol Nidrei	Bruch
	Carlo Fischer	
Vocal	"C'est des Contrabandiers" from Carmen	Bizet
	Mrs. Jeanette M. Lamberton, Winona	
	Marc D. Lombard, At the Piano	
Trio	For Piano, Violin, and Cello, Op. 63	Schumann
	Energico e con passione	
	Vivace, ma non troppo	
	Adagio, con molto affettuoso sentimento	
	Con fuoco	
	Miss Ella Richards, Maximilian Dick, Carlo Fischer	

A Typical Convention Concert

James A. Bliss at the 1911 convention as depicted by Rawson

membered all too well the unsuccessful attempts of 1887 and consequently campaigned to reach all teachers of music both by letter and by notices in the *Western Musical Herald* and in the national magazine, *The Musical Courier*. One distinguished member, Robert Griggs Gale,[19] reported MMTA's activities in the weekly *Bellman*, voice of "cultured" Minneapolis, a magazine which sold as far afield as London and Paris.

Each year brought a successful meeting. Programs took place in churches, institutions with pipe organs and with space enough to hold concert audiences. Beyond the president's address and business meetings, a typical convention program showcased the musicians in two concerts: those by State Talent[20] and by Minnesota Composers.

Where possible, performers were drawn from the sponsoring city not only because of convenience but also because the association was dedicated to statewide work. In accordance with the national policy of a chain of command, county vice-presidents and local leaders had their own session during a convention.

Sandwiched between concerts and business meetings were various papers and roundtables devoted to piano, organ, violin, vocal and public school topics such as "Artistic Singing," "The British Organ," "Music and the Child." Such workshops had permanent value both to members in attendance and those who read the *Annual Reports*. Discussions, the backbone of each convention, became at times impassioned as well as instructive. During one meeting, a lively critique of vocal training arose between the church choir directors who considered themselves experts on boys' voices and the public school music teachers who were directing boys' choruses. At the 1910 convention, the organ workshop became so intense that participants almost missed a new-fangled treat, an "auto ride" that the Mankato sponsors tendered.

During this early period, despite a few such quarrels, no significant divisions existed among the various types of teachers. Members could be college and conservatory teachers, private teachers, organists and choir directors, professional performers, or school music supervisors. Piano teachers were in the majority—not surprising because the piano could reproduce in essence the whole musical fabric and thus was the open sesame to all study.

Women constituted two-thirds of the membership. Music at this time was considered a feminine calling. Carleton College Conservatory, in its first thirty years, graduated only one male student. Macalester College based its decision to admit women in large part on the revenue which would come from fathers eager to have their daughters acquire music.

For some time prior to the twentieth-century, the art had been considered an "accomplishment," something that created what James Huneker called the "piano girl" who cultivated music for "social display."[21] An advertisement in the *Annual Report* for 1906 gives a glimpse of this phenomenon, an outlook in direct opposition to MMTA professional ideals.

This piano firm found quickly that music as coquetry was a thing of the past. Truly devoted MMTA members were less interested in showy "solos" and more in serious "sonatas." Within a year, the firm dropped its "way to a man's heart" and its cupid in favor of more dignified advertisements.

David Ferguson Colville

Hamlin Hunt

Women of the emerging twentieth century found their public fulfillment in teaching and in numerous clubs—many associated with the Minnesota branches of the National Federation of Women's Clubs or the National Federation of Musical Clubs and other groups with worthy purposes. Some of these were completely devoted to music—such as the Brainerd Musical Club, Schumann Club of Fergus Falls, Schubert Club of St. Paul, Thursday Musical of Minneapolis, Mozart Club of St. James, Musical Art Club of Little Falls, the Matinée Musicale or Cecilians of Duluth—but general reading and literary clubs had strong musical programs as well.[22]

Women of MMTA, in many positions of leadership, worked hard for the cause; however, the highest office, that of president, was filled invariably by men. While it may have seemed more natural at that time and within a mixed sex group to place men in the presidency, it was done also as a means of publicity, a luster to be gained from prominent public figures such as David Colville,[23] "tall, handsome, and courteous, a great favorite," teacher in exclusive schools, one of the most popular singers of the day. At least one of these early leaders, Hamlin Hunt,[24] the first Minnesota-born president, brought with him not only local but national acclaim as well. He had already appeared as organ soloist at two World's Fairs by the time that he became MMTA president.

MMTA was dependent upon a small and distinguished cadre of leaders to keep the organization alive, to foster its ideals and to arrange for the time of renewal that came with each yearly convention. Though these dignitaries added renown to the group, both leaders and members really wanted public recognition of the profession, not just distinction for outstanding individuals.

MMTA had, by the end of its first decade, forged links that connected the experienced teacher with the inexperienced, the large musical center with the outlying small town. Beyond the Twin Cities, the association had held conventions in Duluth, Winona, St. Peter, Mankato and Detroit [Lakes]; consequently citizens throughout the state began to recognize the message and standards of MMTA. Despite this, the membership remained at a low level compared to the population of the state—a modest 10 to 12 percent of some 1,800 musicians and music teachers reported on the 1900 census or the same percentage of 3,000 reported in 1910.[25] Still MMTA's influence was proportionately higher because it included the leaders in the profession: the foremost organists, college and conservatory teachers, public school music supervisors, and community performers.

The first years of the twentieth century brought profound changes in the musical life of Minnesota and with them a propitious time for MMTA. Before 1900 most listeners were unschooled in concert music. They enjoyed the entertainment style and tolerated a mixture of that with more serious styles. The Danz Orchestra, for instance, played such things as Labitsky's *Dream on the Alps* alongside helpings of Beethoven, Schumann, Bizet and Wagner. Some unwilling listeners protested that the "very great majority of individuals are not educated up to a standard of classical music, and it becomes a bore to them." The public, and to some extent teachers themselves, had been raised upon what the historian of the Minneapolis Symphony aptly called "caramel-stuffed programs."[26]

Brilliant and picturesque piano solos were well received and the most popular such as Charles Kunkel's *Alpine Storm* were transcribed for band as well. Kunkel's musical idyl[27] tells the story of a shepherd boy piping to his love oblivious of a growing storm. After gradually louder peals in the low bass of the piano, suddenly:

> A terrific thunder clash is to be heard. This is effected with the
> palm of the left hand in the bass, *fff,* all the keys possible—after
> which the roll of the thunder continues as written. This crash,
> well executed, produces an immense effect.

The storm grows in intensity and then gradually fades away and the "sun appears, the birds twitter in the branches, the shepherd again calls his dogs and takes his sheep to pasture and resumes his love song." This required little sophistication on the part of the listener; he or she had only to listen to a single tune and various effects: twitters, crashes, and trills.

Shortly after 1900, a gradual change of taste occurred as listeners began to hear enough "classical music" to be able to accept that style. The transi-

Ruth Anderson and Wilma Anderson, Brussels, 1896–1900

tion is vividly illustrated in the career of Wilma Anderson, one of the most gifted and active MMTA members. In the 1890s she appeared as the "Petite Pianiste" and used Kunkel's *Alpine Storm* as her show piece. After 1900—now grown and returned from a European education—she began playing Beethoven sonatas in public, and by 1914 she gave the Minneapolis premiere of the Rachmaninoff Second Piano Concerto.

Teachers of MMTA joined Miss Anderson in leading the procession toward a "high art" repertory. Most prominent of all, Emil Oberhoffer[28] founded the Minneapolis Symphony in 1903. Keenly aware of the necessity of educating the public, he established a series of Sunday events, the Popular Concerts[29] to bridge the gap between the "caramel-stuffed" repertory and more demanding extended compositions. For these Sunday events, Oberhoffer hired soloists of MMTA: violinists Heinrich Hoevel and William MacPhail, organist Hamlin Hunt and singers Jessica DeWolf, J. Austin Williams, and Harry Phillips.

By 1911 MMTA had successfully joined forces with women's clubs and community leaders to raise public awareness of culture music,[30] the best class of music.[31] The Musical Gibraltar seemed in sight. Dismay and disorder that doomed earlier attempts at organization had given way to vitality and promise. No longer was it necessary for the association to sponsor concerts by nationally-recognized artists. The community had many voices. President Fairclough marveled:

George Fairclough

We musicians of Minnesota can well be proud of the splendid
showing of our state in the musical advancement of the country.
What other state in the Union has two such Symphony
Orchestras as we have? Either one would be a credit to any city
on the continent. Think of the artists we have had in the Twin
Cities this past season. I venture to say that, taking St. Paul and
Minneapolis as one musical center, we have had more symphony
concerts and recitals by famous artists than any other one city in
the country, excepting only New York, Boston and Chicago.[32]

Only one group remained without consistent support: Minnesota composers.
MMTA moved to remedy that situation. It decided to become the voice of
local creative artists; the initial step in what was to be a long-running commitment to composition that has persisted up to the present day.

2

America Must Look to the West for her Composers

In the fallow years between 1887 and 1901 when MMTA remained only an aspiration, two founding members, Willard Patton and Gustavus Johnson,[1] instituted a series of concerts by local composers. Eventually their efforts led to a loosely-constituted group of around twenty-five men and women active between 1890 and 1930, a band of musicians that can be called The First School of Minnesota Composers.

Patton, Johnson and their colleagues had so inspired others that President Clarance Marshall at the first MMTA convention could boast that:

> America must look to the west for her great original composers, the eastern writers reflecting too strongly the influence of European schools. This shows us our responsibilities, and proves that we have a standing already which is sufficient to lead to large future expectations.

Johnson settled in the state permanently in 1880 and Patton in 1883. Both had had fine training and good models in composition—Patton from such teachers as Carl Zerrahn of Boston and Dudley Buck of New York City, and Johnson from such teachers as Johan Gustav Nordquist and Gustav Adolph Mankell of Stockholm. Both looked to their adopted state as a place of unlimited opportunity, a locale for distinguished students and public acclaim. In the season of 1889–1890 they brought major works to the public.

In mid-October, Patton presented at the Minneapolis Grand Opera House a comic opera, *La Fianza,* rich in its orchestration for wind instruments and lavish in costumes and scenery.[2] In the winter, Johnson presented a concert notable not only for the fact that it was a "one-man" show but also because it presented several of the major performers of the Twin Cities and "brought out" the soprano, Olive Fremstad, destined for an international career as leading singer of the Munich Opera and the Metropolitan Opera.[3]

Gustavus Johnson

Johnson's Third Musical Evening of the Season
Dyer Music Hall, 14 February 1890

Polonaise for Piano (four hands)   Johnson
Messrs. Woodruff and Johnson

Fantasie on Swedish Airs, Cello Solo   Johnson
Mr. Schlachter

a. Five Characteristic Pieces   Johnson
b. Nocturne
G. Johnson

"Daffodils"   Johnson
Mr. Porter

Reverie, Violin Solo   Johnson
Swedish Dance, Violin Solo
Mr. Straka

"Thou'rt Near Me"   Johnson
Two Little Swedish Songs
Miss Fremstad

Easter Anthem, Double Quartet   Johnson
Soprano solo by Miss Ulmer

Grand Trio in C   Johnson
Messrs. Johnson, Straka, and Schlachter

Rounding out the season in April, the Danz Orchestra gave a concert, "Music by Home Composers," which presented further compositions by Patton and Johnson with the addition of a few pieces by Gurney, Shuey and Baldamos.

Such stirrings of American creativity were sweeping not only the Gateway to the Great Northwest but the nation as well. New York founded a Manuscript Club in 1889. Minnesota followed quickly with one in 1893, three years before Chicago organized its club. Beyond the realm of music, the decade of the 1890s witnessed the birth of many items of Americanization—the Pledge of Allegiance, Flag Day, the Star Spangled Banner as national anthem, plus several patriotic associations: the Colonial Dames of America, the Daughters of the American Revolution, the U.S. Daughters of 1812, and the Society of Mayflower Descendants.[4] Why should not music also take its place as a national icon? Many of those musicians who studied "abroad" had returned not as newly-made Europeans but as missionaries—their own word—who wanted to build an American musical culture as worthy as that of the old world but expressive of the ideals of the new. The country, coming of age by 1893, was determined to show the world the vigor of America. Its showcase was to be the World Columbian Exposition on Chicago's lakefront. For this great festival, Johnson composed a Piano Concerto on Swedish Airs; however, as it turned out, the Chicago fair had such a crowded schedule that his concerto had to wait some years for its premiere.

At this auspicious moment when the tides of Americanism were running high, Minnesota chose to inaugurate its Manuscript Club with a program by those composers who would later be MMTA members.[5]

Program of the Minnesota Manuscript Club
Studio Hall, Minneapolis, 9 November 1893

Quartet "Dream Song"   Clarance A. Marshall
    from "Prince and Paradise" by Alice I. Norcross
Male Quartet
R. D. Finel, O. J. DeSale, C. E. Fisher, W. H. Eichman

Song for High Soprano   Willard Patton
    "Awake" (Barry Cornwall)
Miss Mattie Redlon

Sonata for Violin and Piano   Gustavus Johnson
Claude Madden and Mr. Johnson

Bass aria from "Triumph of Love"   Samuel A. Baldwin
Charles E. Fisher

Songs: Willam Mentor Crosse
    "Sweet and Low" (Tennyson)
      and other Tennyson songs
    "Unless"
Miss Fannie McLeod

Songs: Clarance A. Marshall
    "Love for Thee"
    "Beware" (Longfellow)
Miss Esther Butler

Quartets for Ladies Voices   Willard Patton
    "When Evening's Twilight"
    "The Maiden's Rose"
Sappho Ladies' Quartet

Song for Soprano   Gustavus Johnson
    "Two Red Roses"
(Originally composed for Miss Maud Ulmer)
Miss McKay

Part Song—Selected   Samuel A. Baldwin
Chorus of Mixed Voices

Following this came a veritable flood of local programs sponsored by the Schubert Club of St. Paul and the Thursday Musicale of Minneapolis.[6]

In the midst of this encouraging public attention, Patton set to work on a large-scale oratorio, *Isaiah,* given "at the Metropolitan Opera House, Minneapolis, 17 January 1897, with a chorus of 225, the Danz orchestra and competent soloists." This work was destined to have a career.

> It proved a great and impressive success and has throughout the years established itself as one of the finest and most popular of American oratorios. In the following year it was given at the great exposition in Omaha with a Minneapolis chorus of 250 taken down there by special train. A wonderful performance was given with the Theodore Thomas festival orchestra for the instrumental support. Five editions of the work have been sold out and performances of it have been given in more than 60 cities.[7]

Shortly after the oratorio, Patton assumed the directorship of the Philharmonic Club of Minneapolis which performed yet two more of his large-scale works—termed musical epics—*The Star of India* and *Footstones of a Nation.*

The decade concluded with another Home Composer's Concert sponsored by the Thursday Musicale presented "as an encouragement to the composers of Minneapolis." In this concert Johnson's piano concerto at last reached performance and *The Minneapolis Times* reported:

> The honors of the evening were conceded by musician and layman to belong to Gustavus Johnson for his piano concerto. It is a composition worthy of hearing anywhere, and would make an impression wherever given. It revealed not only originality, but careful thought. The themes suggested by Swedish folk songs, are full of melody and finely developed. The "Adagio movement" is so spontaneous, so full of exquisite harmonies, and rarely beautiful melody that it seems an inspiration, an outpouring of true musical feeling and soul. The allegro movements are brilliant, and the "Allegro giocoso" works up into a magnificent climax, broad and telling. It is a very symmetrical work and the orchestra and piano are extremely well balanced. It is a composition that offers great opportunities for the pianist.[8]

W.S.B. Mathews was astounded at this program and concluded, from afar in the Windy City, that it must have been a surpassing achievement.

If it is any comfort to the Minneapolis Ladies' Club, the present
reviewer will add the information that in all likelihood this was
the best manuscript program ever given in the United States, sav-
ing possibly unremembered performances of the New York Manuscript Society. Here was a good orchestra (one hopes it was good),
a piano concerto with orchestra, some part songs and a variety
of other compositions, which whatever their merits, pleased the
audience.[9]

Mathews was impressed by the number of large-scale works produced by the
Minnesotans. Most composers around the nation—with the exception of musicians of Boston and New York—were content to produce small songs and
piano pieces. Here was something greater. Patton had composed a successful
oratorio, a genre that was considered to be for the musician "the exact analogy of what the Cathedral is to the Architect—the highest Art-form to the
construction of which he can aspire."[10] Soon another one of these cathedrals
of music was premiered. In April of 1906, J. Victor Bergquist imported
soloists from the East to join his chorus of 250 voices and the Minneapolis
Symphony in a grand performance of his *Golgotha,* a work conceived after
his attendance at the Passion Play during his student days in Europe. Like
Patton's, it was performed in a number of cities but never reached the popu-
larity of the earlier oratorio.

The leading composers of the First Minnesota School, Patton, Johnson,
and Bergquist, were active in MMTA. Each served as president. With their
place in the esteem of musicians and public, it is not surprising that the organization became the sponsor of Minnesota composition. The first convention in
1902 featured performances of Gerard Tonning's *Romanze* for violoncello[11]
and Gertrude Sans Souci's song, *Wishes.*[12] By its second year, MMTA began
scheduling an annual Concert of Minnesota Composers for the delight of
both regular MMTA members and associate members of the public. The program of 1903 is given opposite.

MMTA Minnesota Composers Concert
Plymouth Congregational Church, 8 May 1903

| Piano | a) Novellette | Arthur Bergh |
| | b) Appassionata | (St. Paul) |

Miss Minnie Bergh (St. Paul)

Violin	Sonata in G Major	Claude Madden
	Moderato assai	(St. Paul)
	Allegro grazioso	
	Andante affetuoso	
	Allegro energico	

Arthur Bergh (St. Paul)
Miss Minnie Bergh at the piano

Songs	a) The Year's First Crocus	John Parsons Beach
	b) Shadow and Gleam	(Minneapolis)
	c) The Wind on the Wold	
	d) All in a Garden	
	e) The Moon of Roses	
	f) 'Twas in a World of Living Leaves	

William Herbert Dale (Minneapolis)
Mr. Beach at the piano

| Violin | Intermezzo | Carlyle Scott |
| | | (Minneapolis) |

Mrs. Carlyle Scott (Minneapolis)
Mr. Scott at the piano

Songs	a) When Song is Sweet	Gertrude Sans Souci
	b) Wishes	(Minneapolis)
	c) Thoughts	

Mrs. W. N. Porteous (Minneapolis)
Miss Sans Souci at the piano

Violin	"In Venice," Suite Moderne	Gerard Tonning
	Morning	(Duluth)
	In the Old Palace	
	Minuet	
	Gondoliero	
	Carnival	

Carl Riedelsberger (Minneapolis)
Mr. Tonning at the piano

Songs	a) The Arrow and the Quiver	David Ferguson Colville
	b) An Autumn Song	(St. Paul)
	c) By the Splendor in the Heaven	

Miss Alberta Fisher (Minneapolis)
Franklyn Krieger (St. Paul) at the piano

| Piano | Song Without Words | Marc D. Lombard |
| | | (Winona) |

Mr. Lombard

Recit. and Aria		Willard Patton
	"Come near, ye Nations" (Isaiah)	(Minneapolis)
	"Of Thee" (Romanza)	

Harry E. Phillips (St. Paul)
Mrs. A. P. Thomes (Minneapolis) at the piano.

Such home-grown programs became so popular that the planners put them first on the convention agenda since they attracted a full house.[13]

During the ensuing years MMTA brought to the public, in total, the following compositions by forty composers:

> 117 songs
>   including 2 male quartets, 3 women's quartets, and 1 mixed
>   quartet
> 38 piano pieces including 3 sonatas and 1 concerto mvt.
> 20 string pieces
>   including several sonatas, 2 trios, 2 quartets, 1 piano quintet,
>   1 violin concerto, and a suite for strings
> 10 organ pieces
> 1 Te Deum
> 1 anthem
> 1 melodrama

We can marvel at the devotion, energy and accomplishments of these musicians but must also admit that from today's perspective they fell short of President Marshall's expectation that "great original composers" would come out of the West. They wrote in the style of the German classicists, perfect in its way but whose possibilities had already been exhausted. Their New England counterparts faced the same impasse. They and the Minnesotans, despite some worthy compositions that would interest today's audience, remain seldom performed. They needed an injection of new blood, a new vigor from folk sources, from popular music, or from more daring systems of harmony and counterpoint.

There were untapped possibilities in Minnesota: songs and dances of the Indian tribes of the state, Scandinavian folk music, or the lively "vernacular" music of the American frontier. Several musicians were studying American Indian music: Frances Densmore of Red Wing,[14] Arthur Farwell[15] of St. Paul, and Stella Stocker[16] of Duluth. These and others preserved a precious heritage but the "Indianist" composers who tried to use the indigenous material did not create a lasting style; the culture of the tribes and the white men being too far apart for an amalgam to be made. Gustavus Johnson used Swedish tunes but more as quotations than as building blocks for an independent compositional style.

Most of the cultivated composers failed to see any possibility of uniting their high style with the music of the people. The public too kept these two styles more or less in separate compartments. Hal Woodruff, conductor of the Apollo Club of Minneapolis, found that his cultivated music went unappreciated. An old man rose and said, "Much obleeged to ye, young fellow, for givin' us this entertainment. We understand your hands needs limberin' up. So now if you're through with them there finger exercises, you might just play us a piece." Woodruff "obleeged" and brought down the house with "Money Musk" and "Johnny Get Your Gun."[17]

None the less the Minnesotans achieved some notable results. Their compositions were solidly, very correctly written and organized. Such musical precision would have been impossible without MMTA composer-members versed in the theory of music. Among those represented on the program above, Beach was a graduate of the New England Conservatory; Scott had been a harmony student in Leipzig of Jadassohn, one of the most renowned theorists of the world; and Tonning had studied in Munich with Rheinberger, mentor to large numbers of Americans at this time. Each had a basic knowledge of music theory that distinguished them as the founders of MMTA from the run-of-the-mill teachers who could offer only finger exercises and salon compositions.

If they did not write for the ages, they did raise the taste of their contemporaries through showing that American music was worthy of attention, that Minnesotans should aspire to be leaders not just in the community but in the wider musical world, and that musicians should be trained not only in performance but in a fundamental theoretical knowledge of their art.

❧

Carlyle Scott

Carlyle McRoberts Scott, who for the past five years has made a speciality of piano work abroad, announces to the musical public that he is to make Minneapolis and St. Paul his headquarters and field of instruction.

Mr. Scott began his work in Germany with a prominent pupil of Eugene D'Albert, and for the past two years has been an assistant to Robert Teichmueller, one of the leading piano pedagogues of Leipzig.

Of his work in this capacity, and as a soloist, Herr Teichmueller writes:

Mr. Carlyle Scott is a very gifted pianist, who for the past two years has continued his studies under my guidance with the greatest success. His playing is marked by a full, singing tone, dramatic temperament and intelligent interpretation. Also as my assistant, Mr. Scott has shown himself well qualified as an instructor, having very carefully prepared pupils for my classes in a manner entirely to my satisfaction.

Robert Teichmueller
Teacher at the Royal Conservatory of Leipzig

On April 1st, 1901, Mr. Scott will open his studio in the Metropolitan Music Co.'s building. Arrangements for lessons may be made daily, from 3 to 5 P.M.
Special classes in Harmony and Counterpoint.

Scott's Publicity Brochure

3

Help Us All to be Giants

"MMTA will help us all to be giants indeed—with our heads among the clouds but with our feet treading very practical earth." So wrote Wilma Anderson, editor of *Minnesota Music,* the association's magazine, as she summed up the results of the Thirteenth Convention. The members understood immediately the musical ideals that led to heads among the clouds just as they recognized the practical issues: how does one evaluate teachers, how does one make them known in the community, and how does one give them professional status?

In the nineteenth century, music teachers were frequently called "professor." This honorary title seemed appropriate to what was considered a "cultivated" or even "divine" art. In the twentieth century, this almost-automatic designation began to pale as the public compared musicians with a growing number of degree-holding professors in other disciplines. Degrees in medicine were universal. Degrees in music were rare. Musicians had at the most a certificate from a conservatory. Many, however, had studied privately with well-known artists but they could only present to the public a recommendation.[1]

Such a testimonial sometimes became part of a personal brochure which introduced the teacher to the community as it did in the case of Carlyle Scott.[2] Note that he gave special classes in music theory so essential to a complete understanding of music and musical composition. His brochure carried his photo on the cover, an image that transformed his youthful, boyish looks into the figure of a dignified professional man.

His letter of recommendation is only one of many garnered by members of MMTA. The list of their European teachers in the later decades of the nineteenth century and the first decade of the twentieth reads like an honor role of fabled musicians—Philipp, Guilmant, Ysaÿe, Ševčik, Moszkowski, Jadassohn, Riemann, and many others. Minnesota had a strong contingent in Europe—two students in Brussels, one in London, two in Prague, and almost forty in Germany.[3] Other recommendations, especially in the early days when

Yankee pioneers opened up Minnesota, came from teachers in New York and Boston.

Yet those who had studied abroad tended to be favored.[4] Their privileged position had perhaps a bit of snobbery about it but it also came from the kind of aspiration they brought back from their European experiences. Having encountered a thriving musical life, they yearned to establish a similar love of music in Minnesota. They returned as missionaries to bring art to their communities, to build ideals such as MMTA's overriding purpose: "to promote the true culture of music."[5]

Certificates and recommendations worked well for some teachers but for many aspiring teachers unable to afford foreign study or even extended study with a great master there remained a need for something concrete to establish their credentials. It was essential that MMTA find a means of assuring the quality of its teachers—and in a way that would be apparent to the public.

The national organization had no immediate plan for certifying teachers. An earlier plan of 1884–1895 for an American College of Musicians, based on the system used by the British Royal College of Organists, had dwindled. None the less, the British system of strict examinations for three ranks, Licentiate, Associate, and Fellow, remained the model to which musicians and public looked.

When the MMTA took up the cause in 1911, they naturally looked once again toward the Royal College and a similar organization, the Incorporated Society of Musicians of Great Britian and Ireland. They also had before them a more recent association, the American Guild of Organists, AGO, itself based on British principles. Minnesotans even had a local exemplar: the Minnesota Chapter of AGO[6] organized in 1910 by MMTA member, George Fairclough.[7]

All of these associations, British and American, had testing programs leading to certificates for members at various degrees of proficiency: the Licentiate at the lowest level, Associate at the middle level, and Fellow at the highest level. With these models in mind, MMTA members plunged into a struggle for certification, an effort that exacted a great toll upon members. At the Eleventh Convention, 1912, President Thornton[8] had to retire on the final day because he "felt indisposed and fatigued from the strenuous work preparing for the meeting." In the following year at the Twelfth Convention, President Heinrich Hoevel[9] presided over "the most extensive and exhausting business meeting ever held by the association."

The plan to stimulate teachers and inform the public had been brewing for a long time. Patton, a pioneer leader, believed that "those who do not enrich their minds through study will surely become stale as teachers, while those

George A. Thornton

Heinrich Hoevel

pursuing the opposite course will not only remain fresh and resourceful, but will grow and develop."[10] He held that such "higher musicianship must result in greater efficiency in the studio and wider influence in the community."[11]

"Musicianship" had been one of the main concerns of both the national and the state organizations. As early as the year before MMTA was founded, Mrs. Strong of Albert Lea, Minnesota, had called upon the national organization to establish a "recognized standard," and in 1905, Willard Patton had asked his Minnesota colleagues to "inaugurate a series of examinations."[12] Finally in 1909, MMTA started what became "three years of searching debate on this delicate and vital subject," a discussion which Patton said "discovered hidden talent and unhorsed cavorting mediocrity."[13] At the end of this gestation period, a procedure was proposed for three ranks similar to those of the Organists Guild.

The certification plan came to a vote at the convention of 1912 during the tenure of President George Thornton, well-known organist of St. Paul. The program committee of that year realized that an inspirational speaker would speed approval and so chose Charles Henry Mills, head of the Music Department of the University of Illinois, a shining example of the British system of certification: Fellow of the Royal College of Organists, Associate of the Royal College of Music, and Doctor of Music from McGill University in Canada.

Mills told the delegates that the Minnesota plan would remedy many of the deficiencies of the unregulated system existing in the United States. While he recognized many imperfections among the rank and file of music teachers, he still viewed America as the "promised land" with large numbers of music departments, good teachers, fine orchestras and a school of composition bound to bear wondrous fruit. His vision incorporated the principle long-established in both national and state groups of a professional chain linking musical leaders to local teachers: "We can make the metropolis of each state a centre of musical activity from which that of the other cities will radiate."[14]

Heeding his call for music to "radiate" and crowning the long years of preparation, MMTA approved their comprehensive plan "with the utmost enthusiasm, and then, by a rising vote, every member pledged himself to take the examination at the appointed time."[15] Ernest Kroeger of St. Louis sent a congratulatory telegram from his state where a more tentative plan was beginning. The Voice Teachers Guild of Minneapolis sent their approval and a pledge to be the first to take "any fair and practical examination." A triumph!

To put teeth into its actions, the executive board persuaded the members to incorporate the association. Conservatories, associations, and even churches were seeking state incorporation papers. To be able to write "incorporated" after a name gave the public an assurance of status. More than anything it conveyed a guarantee of permanence and continuity. Consequently, the three ranking officers of MMTA drew up Articles of Incorporation which were filed with the Secretary of State 20 October 1913.

A new Constitution had to be written with the principal aims and purposes spelled out clearly. Some items had to be shifted to the By-Laws. Great care was necessary because the fundamentals spelled out in the Articles of Incorporation were not subject to easy change.

The association retained its original aims—"to promote the true culture of music by the interchange of ideas, to advance the interests of musical art and to foster professional fraternity," aims which combined the idealistic with the practical—or what Wilma Anderson called "the very practical earth" and the "heads among the clouds." To accomplish these principles, the First Article of Incorporation spelled out seven actions:

> [1] to establish . . . local musical organizations, [2] to publish . . .
> a musical journal, [3] to issue certificates of learning and profi-
> ciency, [4] to hold an annual convention, [5] to purchase or convey
> any real estate or personal property, [6] to exercise the ordinary
> powers of corporations and [7] to do all things necessary . . . to ac-
> complish the purpose of its organization.

At the same time, the group dropped the word "state" from its official title. They terminated the membership category that allowed the public to buy tickets to convention programs—the word *associate* was now reserved for the second-highest degree of certification. Finally they abandoned the concept of county groups in favor of nine districts, a practice similar to today's plan.

From the very beginning members had realized the value of public announcements. Consequently in 1906 they had decided to make the Des Moines-Chicago journal, the *Western Musical Herald,*[16] their "official organ." Now in 1913 as a newly-incorporated association embarking on an accreditation plan and producing thoughtful essays in its *Annual Reports,* MMTA decided to go one step further and publish its own magazine, *Minnesota Music,* a bimonthly, which began to appear in November of that year.

The magazine, supported in part by advertisements by local and national firms, flourished for a year or two but gradually deadlines were missed and contributions dried up. Some issues were omitted and by 1917, the executive board voted to suspend publication. For the next four years, the *Annual Report* was issued under the title of *Minnesota Music* but the idea of an "official organ" was abandoned until the *Northwest Musical Herald* was founded in 1927.

Leopold G. Bruenner

By now, MMTA had achieved a new structure and outlook. The organization was filled with euphoria. Hard work on the part of the Board of Examiners,[17] leaders and members followed. MMTA wisely called upon presidents who could lead with grace and persuasion. The first of these was Leopold Bruenner,[18] well-known as the director of a select group, the Choral Arts Society, which at this time was performing a much larger repertory than usual—from Renaissance to Twentieth Century styles. To Bruenner fell the task of inspiring the members in their first full year under the new rules—a job which he managed so well that, at the picnic following the convention, he was awarded the Medal of Prince of Good Fellows. Winners of the other awards such as those for the Pie Eating Contest, Fat Ladies Race, and Ham Chewing Contests had best be left unidentified!

Bruenner was followed by three outstanding leaders, William MacPhail,[19] a go-getter who was just organizing his own school of music; Harry Phillips,[20] exceptional baritone and conductor; and J. Austin Williams,[21] Director of the Wesley Methodist Church Choir. MacPhail brought Mrs. Marian Nevins MacDowell, widow of the famed composer, and John Freund, editor of

William MacPhail

J. Austin Williams

HARRY PHILLIPS
Basso Cantante
PUPIL OF OSCAR SEAGLE
Director and Soloist of the
Westminster Presbyterian Church Choir
Director of Macalester College of Music
ORATORIO AND SONG RECITALS
Studio: 507 METROPOLITAN MUSIC BUILDING

Harry Phillips' Professional Card

PRINCIPAL NOTES OF MINNESOTA
MUSIC TEACHERS' DIATONIC SCALE

"DO"
WILLARD PATTON

"SOL"
E N FERGUSON

"MI"
LEOPOLD BRUENER

"DO"
MISS MABEL FULTON

Cartoon by Rawson

Musical America to inspire members to redouble their efforts to support American music. Phillips introduced the group to wide-ranging repertory—from a Bach Cantata to a special discussion of modern music. Williams brought a special interest in music for youth and for operettas.

The public, well aware of these noted leaders, was becoming fascinated with MMTA. The musical movers and shakers even became subjects for the popular cartoons of the day: here Patton, Ferguson, Bruenner and the Duluth piano teacher, Mabel Fulton.

After this grueling period which in the space of a few months had seen MMTA transformed by new membership requirements, a new constitution, articles of incorporation, and a new publication, came a period of recovery in which, unfortunately, some of the initial enthusiasm evaporated. The association launched a publicity campaign to educate the public and entice teachers to apply. As with any new-born, problems arose. The first tests for the Certificate of Licentiate were conducted 5 July 1913 in Minneapolis, St. Paul, Duluth and Winona—a tiring day for all concerned with three hours allotted for Theory and History and another three hours, plus an extension, for the candidate's specialty.

At this point, fundamental difficulties appeared. Most of the mature teachers did not appear. The summer vacation intervened and the Board of Examiners did not finish its grading until fall. Finally, "with a certain strictness in grading," only 57% of the candidates passed. They were rewarded with their certificates carrying the MMTA seal and their names were published in *Minnesota Music*.

The result could only be termed a qualified success. A certain grace period was going to be necessary to advance the plan. Despite the annoying problems of this initial season of testing, the feeling of camaraderie that characterized MMTA did not evaporate and Patton could conclude that Minnesota had an "unusually strong array of highly competent instructors" who could help redeem "America from the art-limbo to which she has been relegated. We believe that the standardization of teachers, in which we have had the honor of trying to lead the way, will be a mighty element in the achievement of this grand result."[22]

Soon requests for information on the "Minnesota Plan" came from state associations in California, Vermont, Missouri, and Louisiana. Within a short time, other states asked guidance. MMTA had shown the way!

Each succeeding year, teachers took the Licentiate Examinations and by 1918, over one hundred state teachers had been certified. Each year, MMTA made brave efforts to schedule tests for the Associate Certificate, the next higher level. Advanced tests were to be conducted by out-of-state experts who had to be paid high fees. Not enough teachers applied to make them feasible. Only twice in the period up to 1918 were the Associate examinations given. The first time, despite examiners of repute, the questions were judged inadequate and not "truly indicative of the grade they were supposed to establish." The second attempt in 1918 fared slightly better with eight applicants. There should have been at least 50 by that point. As early as 1917, a committee at the Winona Convention reported:

> The rest of the plan, providing examinations for the higher certificates, has failed. That the expense of the system is the reason for this failure does not mitigate the failure . . . a partial success of the standardization of teachers up to the Licentiate degree has been attained; the higher ranks of the profession in the state remain as completely unstandardized and un-unified as before.[23]

The ideal of ridding the state of "cavorting mediocrity" remained in part a realization and in part a noble ideal. MMTA in the next decade searched for a solution that would make the plan a complete success.

Minnesota Music Teachers' Association

This is to Certify, That **Thaddeus P. Giddings**.

has satisfactorily complied with the requirements prescribed by this Association for the certificate of

Associate

in

Voice

and is entitled to all attendant honor and privilege.

In Witness Whereof, We have hereunto set our hands and caused the seal of the Association to be affixed, this 8th day of *March* 19 33

J. Austin Williams
Examiner

Gustav Schoettle
Chairman Board of Examiner.

R. Buchanan Morton
President

Esther Jones Gaylor
Secretary

An MMTA Certificate

4

To Issue Certificates of Proficiency and Learning

The musician's task required first the basic talent of remembering tones, melodies, harmonies and textures: what is generally called a "musical ear." Secondly, it required the ability to read printed music easily in order to translate abstract symbols into living tone with appropriate emotional quality and declamatory emphasis. All of this was to be accomplished while engaged in physical motions of extreme dexterity and endurance. All was to be error free. In short, a mental and physical feat! Only with a long period of education, often beginning at a tender age, could all of these details be absorbed and become a fluent musical language as natural as one's native tongue.

Any tests for "certificates of proficiency and learning"[1] had to be equally complex. To satisfy such involved demands, MMTA had agreed on three examinations for each member: one in the candidate's specialty, a second in music theory, and a third in music history, a threefold format drawn from the standards reigning among organists, the comprehensive plan that British-trained George Thornton and other leaders had advocated for the Minnesotans.

Members frequently compared their situation to that of the medical profession. President William MacPhail told the teachers:

> Your physician, and your dentist are both proud of their diplomas, framed and hanging on the wall in the most conspicuous place, certificates of ability, that doctors of unquestionable standing are glad to display, not because they need them to impress their patients, but because of the principle for which they stand.[2]

The analogy was apt. Medical and musical candidates both had to master a staggering amount of detail and an involved combination of the theoretical and the practical.

Each candidate was subject, first of all to the most basic of the three examinations, the specialty examination. Each had to know his or her instrument, its construction and its possibilities; then had to explain many technical details such as the following for pianists:

> *Question 4*
> (a) In your judgment, what is the importance of scale study and practice?
> (b) Give the fingering of the following scales: B major, F major, G sharp melodic minor, E flat minor, B flat minor, C sharp minor.
> (c) Do you give any other than the traditional fingerings for scale and arpeggios?

Beyond such essentials as scale fingerings, bowings, technical studies, and such items, a candidate was expected to indicate in an actual musical example the shading and phrasing that would convey the spirit and artistry of the music. In 1915, for example, pianists were asked the following.

> *Question 5*
> Indicate very minutely the fingering, phrasing, shading and pedaling of the enclosed composition:
>   Moment Musical, F Minor, Op. 94, No. 3 (Schubert)

While the public could readily recognize the value of the specialty examination, it was not as aware of the necessity of music theory. Perhaps more than any other topic, the system of music theory remains even today a mystery to the layman. Bright people are apt to be puzzled by all of this talk of tonics, dominants, second inversions, tonality, chords, two against three, fugal imitation, development and such. Yet the same people would not hesitate to recognize the grammatical system of language.

The layman, looking at a musical score, might think that it could be read note by note. Such an approach would be as impractical as trying to read literature letter by letter. The musician has to recognize immediately the larger units of musical discourse—comparable to the words, phrases, sentences, paragraphs, or even larger units in prose or poetry. It is true that some people can write without knowing a noun from a verb. Still such persons remain limited in what they can produce. Similarly a musician can perform at some levels without knowing music theory but that person often remains only a skillful imitator not capable of independently interpreting works of the past or conveying his own musical ideas to others.

All too frequently a student could be coached by a teacher into a composition, taught note by note or idea by idea. In the early days of MMTA, such coaching was more common than today. It could even result in the $1,000 dollar piece: $1,000 in lessons and one composition to show for it. Even up through the 1930s, a singer with a beautiful voice was frequently coached, not taught. The result, unfortunately, was that, at times, a prompter had to sing whole pages to get the "glorious voice" back on track—an actual occurence on a Metropolitan Opera broadcast. MMTA early took a stand against coaching and insisted upon the kind of knowledge for teachers and students that would lead to independent judgment, the ability to learn on one's own.

Under the influence of founders, composers and thoroughly-educated performers knowledgeable in the art, the standards for music theory examinations were instituted and kept at a high level. The candidate was expected to know basic facts of notation, to define the various Italian terms commonly used, to identify intervals—the distances between notes—and to write scales in various keys and harmonize them. Some clever questions such as the following forced the candidate to know musical theory so well that she or he could correct mistakes in harmony or in rhythmic notation.

Question 5b
Correct this exercise, by changing Alto or Tenor parts, do not alter Treble or Bass.

Question 6a
Rewrite this correctly in accordance with time signature.
The same sound must be retained in your correction.

The third examination for each candidate bore the name of history but it might more aptly have been called an examination in the literature of music. It is true that the candidate was asked to discuss such historical movements as Classicism or Romanticism yet the bulk of this examination asked for definitions of genre types, such as concerto, symphony, etc. Often the examination asked for the identification of composers.

Question 5.
Give a brief sketch of the life of Richard Wagner.
Name three of his greater compositions.

Question 9.
To what nationality and period do the following composers belong and in what form of music was each most successful?

Rossini	Rameau	Debussy	Brahms	Cadman
Berlioz	Gluck	Tschaikowski	Schumann	Chadwick
Handel	St.-Saëns	Stainer	Beach	Hadley

In an age that was still inclined to teach "solos" or "pieces," MMTA tried for a higher standard, for an acquaintance with the great masterpieces, the compositions considered profound and worthy of the divine art. In his or her study for the qualifying examination and in teaching, many a member amassed a considerable library of scores, an essential in an age when concerts were not as frequent and recordings were still in a primitive state. Naturally, the larger the teacher's library, the broader the teacher's background and the more students profited.

This examination for the Licentiate covered what would be found in the first two years of college education in music. The more advanced examinations were designed to move from "fundamental fact" to "experience, judgment, and wide knowledge."[3] including the theory of music through counterpoint and orchestration. Special exceptions to theoretical knowledge were made for singers who, in compensation, had to demonstrate knowledge of languages.

☙❦❧

MINNESOTA MUSIC

VOL. VI   JUNE, 1919   NO. 1

OFFICIAL PROGRAM

Eighteenth Annual Convention

Minnesota Music Teachers' Association

Carleton College   Northfield, Minn.

June 19, 20 and 21, 1919

E.B.

5

The Most Important Era of Musical Development This Country Has Ever Seen

"After the most terrible four years of the world's history, it behooves us musicians to fall in line, keep step with the rest of man's activities, and prepare ourselves for the most important era of musical development this country has ever seen," said President Fairclough—sounding a positive note after the horrors of World War I, the Great War. He presented a number of reasons for hope to MMTA assembled for its eighteenth annual convention in 1919 at Carleton College, Northfield, Minnesota. Among them:

> Where the farmer, a few years ago, provided his daughter with a parlor organ of the foot-pumped variety, today she must have a piano of good make, and he also sees that she takes lessons from the best teacher to be had, possibly a recent graduate of some conservatory, who is located in the near-by town. The flooding of the country with talking machines, player-pianos, etc., has whetted the appetite of the great American people for good music.[1]

Fairclough might well have mentioned not only new musical machines but an impressive array of musical associations which sprang up as the good times rolled:

1916 *National Bureau for the Advancement of Music*
   1) *National Music Memory Contest*
   2) *National School Band Association*
   3) *National School Orchestra Association*
   4) *National Music Week* (1924) in cooperation with the
      National Federation of Music Clubs
1917 *National Music Publishers Association*
1917 *Musical Alliance of America*
1919 *National Association of Music Merchants* formed from the
      older group of Piano Dealers (1902)

1919 *National Association of Negro Musicians*
1924 *National Association of Schools of Music*

The roaring twenties brought new attitudes, new jobs, and new schools. A confidence in America[2] had grown out of wartime experiences. Citizens had found a sort of bond, a conviction that they could accomplish great deeds through civic and national endeavor. As the country moved from war to peace, many of the wartime musical practices were changed into a new endeavor: civic music.

MMTA member Leopold Bruenner's Liberty Chorus transformed itself into a Municipal Chorus, one of the first such groups in the nation. They became quite popular and performed twenty or more concerts a year. As early as 1921, St. Paul sponsored an inspirational Music Week, some three years in advance of the national movement.

> Dedicating this week to Music, it is the desire to have each and every one give a thought each day to music. No one thing so nearly touches us all—no battles have been fought—no victories celebrated—no peace concluded without music. It is the language of love, sorrow, despair, compassion and religion, and most of all has it become an institution in the American home.[3]

By 1924, St. Paul appropriated yearly $25,000 toward its municipal music program, $20,000 for two summer bands, $2,000 toward two winter bands, $2,000 for the Municipal Chorus, and $1,000 for singing and entertainment.[4] Minneapolis had a Civic Music League which by 1920 had 1,100 members. Its leaders met weekly for lunch and discussion.[5] Each city erected a monster auditorium and each hired a municipal organist who gave regular concerts.

Concurrent with burgeoning civic music came new opportunities for employment. First, the movie houses needed organists and pianists who could provide mood music as silent films unrolled; musicians who could lead the audience in sing-alongs, a popular adjunct to the major cinema attraction. Organists even invented a swank word—*photo-playing*—to describe this new vocation.[6]

Second, the pioneer radio stations needed staff pianists and organists such as Ramona Gerhard ("Twenty Flying Fingers"), and Eddy Dunstedter ("at the Mighty Wurlitzer"). They also needed musically knowledgable supervisors such as MMTA member Eleanor Poehler to arrange their programs. As Managing Director of the station WLAG, predecessor of WCCO, she called upon many of her colleagues for live music to be broadcast.

Third the business community needed band, choral, and orchestra leaders because it had decided that music would enhance sales if heard within the store and would also improve employee satisfaction when clerks and other personnel played in company-run performing groups. The Wannamaker Department Store in Philadelphia, a leader in the movement, acquired the largest organ in the world[7] and presented daily organ recitals—a single facet in the store's extensive music program which included as well six bands funded by the company.[8] Minnesota industry, giddy with similar projects,[9] sponsored such groups as the Buzza Ladies Orchestra, Pillsbury Flour Women's Glee Club, Pillsbury Band, Twin City Rapid Transit Quartets, Brown & Bigelow Concert Band and Jazz Orchestra, Emporium Men's Chorus, or the Great Northern Railway choruses, band & orchestra.

Fourth, colleges, conservatories, and universities, thriving in the heated economy and in the midst of a building boom, needed music teachers.[10] The Minneapolis School of Music, Oratory and Dramatic Art boasted in the 1919–1920 season of its new building, "one block from the Auditorium, where the symphony concerts, operas and other leading musical attractions are given."[11] The MacPhail School of Music opened its four-story, fireproof building for the season of 1923–1924 to serve its 140 teachers and 5,000 students.[12] The *Civic and Commerce Bulletin* reported proudly that

> a city that can harbor an orchestra of its own, that can buy a Titian for its museum, that is building one of the largest auditoriums in the world and supports a school of such extension as the MacPhail, may be looked upon as one of the musical centers not only in America, but also in the music world.[13]

The University of Minnesota in a great building frenzy—a stadium, library and huge auditorium—inaugurated its Music Building[14] in the season of 1922–1923 with gala concerts by the Flonzaley and London String Quartets, an Arthur Bodansky staging of *Cosi Fan Tutte* and a gala performance of *Elijah*.

With this cornucopia of riches—civic pride, new jobs, flourishing schools—it seemed to MMTA that the good times might just roll on forever. No one doubted that America had arrived at the "most important era of musical development this country has ever seen."

During the war, MMTA had found itself in straightened condition due to the expense of certifying teachers and of publishing a music magazine. It was particularly difficult to pay for nationally-recognized examiners needed for advanced examinations. By 1917, a deficit had developed and members were being asked to pay their 1918 dues quickly in order to keep MMTA functioning. It seemed that the push to "be giants indeed," might fail. In those

James Lang

pitiful circumstances the organization persuaded, with some difficulty, two former presidents, Hamlin Hunt and George Fairclough, to assume office once again and rescue MMTA from its problems.

Once this had been accomplished, three new leaders, James Lang, Elsie Shawe, and Stanley Avery, ushered the organization into a flourishing period. Lang[15] had already organized a cooperative group of music teachers, the Fine Arts Studio, in Minneapolis and now used his talent to re-energize MMTA. He and his Chairman of the Examining Board, Patton, told the teachers that European professors had great influence because of their "broader and more profound musicianship." They were convinced that Minnesotans too could find something of "inestimable value" in their study of harmony and music history. The hope was that each generation could improve itself and that each succeeding generation might build upon the preceding one. The artist of the future might "stand upon the shoulders of former greatness!"

Elsie Shawe,[16] the group's first woman president, had been a founding member of both MMTA and the Music Supervisor's National Conference. She wanted the members to understand music classes of the public schools and wanted MMTA to merge with the public school teachers. Toward that end, she arranged to have members visit the Minnesota Education Association (MEA), conventions. Not many actually did attend. Those who did found Music placed in the Department of Industrial and Household Arts. What a contrast between MMTA sessions which addressed major musical topics and the MEA sessions which mainly "showcased" student performing groups! This cleft between amateur—in the best sense of that word, "lover"—and professional, between performance for pleasure and serious study of the structure of music was unfortunately to widen with the years.

Elsie Shawe

Stanley Avery with Minnesotans Adair McRae (middle)
and Herbert Elwell (right) at Fontainebleau

Stanley Avery[17] came to MMTA with great fanfare. He was in the midst of founding the choral department of the MacPhail School of Music and he had just returned from the first class at the American Conservatory at Fontainebleau[18] where he, along with Aaron Copland, won honorable mention in composition. It was in his term that the impasse created between the rank-and-file and the advocates of certification reached a crisis point.

Lang, Shawe, and Avery, all three, realized that unless a large number of members were certified, MMTA would not thrive. The membership at the end of the war stood only at around 150, not significantly greater than the 133 members of 1902. For nearly three years, 1919–1921, the association debated various ways of certification that would attract members. Finally, at the convention of 1922, they voted—against considerable opposition—to allow teachers to be certified by affidavit instead of by examination.

Each applicant had to fill out a three-page questionnaire listing his or her general education and musical training, repertory, and teaching experience. This was to be notarized and then filed with the Secretary of State if first adjudged sufficient by the MMTA Examiner's Board. This plan successfully "grandfathered in" about all the truly qualified teachers at the Licentiate level, saved the organization large sums for examinations, and raised the membership to better levels.

After this crucial turning point in 1922, R. Buchanan Morton,[19] organist and voice teacher, took over the president's post. Under his presidency and the presidencies of his successors, Donald Ferguson and J. Victor Bergquist,

R. Buchanan Morton

MMTA caught the roaring spirit of the new age. Administrative activity was doubled.[20] Members came pouring in.

A new spirit of professionalism appeared in the musical programs of the conventions. Up to this point six to eight members had presented a miscellany of pieces, the State Talent Program. Now MMTA began to ask only one or two performers or a chamber ensemble to present a program in the format of a professional solo concert, the sort of thing that would be heard in the concert hall or on the radio.[21]

Joint Recital at the Nineteenth Annual Convention
22 June 1920, Unitarian Church, Minneapolis

La Procession	César Franck
Le Colibri	Chausson
Le Temps des Fées	Koechlin

Eleanor Poehler, Soprano
Louise Chapman, Accompanist

Sonata, Opus 36	Rachmaninow
Allegro agitato	
Lento	
Allegro molto	

Harrison Wall Johnson, Pianist

Mr. Silversmith	Old Spanish
To a Hill Top	Ralph Cox
A Monotone	Cornelius
Rain	Pearl Curran
There is No Death	O'Hara

Eleanor Poehler

Sphinx	Cyril Scott
Lotus Land	Cyril Scott
La Plus que Lente	Debussy
L'Isle joyeuse	Debussy

Harrison Wall Johnson

Children's Songs for Grown People—	
A Fairy-Tale Lullaby	Henry Hadley
Grandma's Prayer	Hageman
The Mystic	Chadbourne
Concerning Love	Chadbourne
Swinging	Foster
The Froggies Lullaby	McGhie

Eleanor Poehler

Though MMTA had attracted national attention through its certification program and had supported American composition, it was only in 1921, under the leadership of Shawe, that the group entered into an official affiliation with the national association, MTNA. From this time on, Minnesotans joined wholeheartedly in the Americanization movement. Guests of national renown—such as Leopold Auer or Josef Lhevinne—were invited to state conventions for artist recitals and for teaching advice. Members began to attend the national conventions regularly.

It was at the national meeting at Dayton, Ohio, in 1925, that MMTA President Donald Ferguson[22] first presented to the public his explanation of the expressive quality of music, that quality which members recognized as

Donald N. Ferguson

essential if difficult to define. He drew upon psychology to show how music expressed emotion, how it went beyond mere grammar and aesthetic qualities of beauty until it revealed itself as a: "real and priceless language [that] gives lucid and intelligible expression to the 'feeling-tone' of mature and pondered experience."[23] He continued to expound his ideas at both state and national levels for the next fifty years and, in doing so, gave both groups a soundly-reasoned pride in their art and profession.

The crowning point of this entrance into the American movement came when Minnesota hosted the national convention in December of 1927. The year before, MTNA had celebrated its fiftieth anniversary at Rochester, New York. Members in the East expressed doubt that a successful convention could be held as far west as Minneapolis. Minnesotans took this as a challenge and produced a lively convention with the "largest attendance of recent years." MMTA led the enrollment with 266 Minnesota teachers out of a total of 658 delegates!

The local program committee showcased the finest in Minnesota talent: the Verbrugghen String Quartet, the Minneapolis Symphony Orchestra, and the St. Olaf Choir. Out-of-towners found the performance of Eunice Norton in the Rachmaninoff Second Piano Concerto "outstanding" and the concert of the St. Olaf Choir a thing of "rare beauty." Several Minnesotans addressed the convention: Mr. H. A. Bellows, the manager of radio station WCCO, spoke on "Musical Education by Radio," Lotus D. Coffman, the president of the University of Minnesota, on "Antidotes of Industrialism," and Carolyn Bowen of the MacPhail School on "The Modern Piano Teacher, an Educator."

MTNA was an umbrella organization that drew its participants from every area of musical endeavor: college and conservatory teachers, scientists, librarians, historians, public school officials, composers, editors and publishers. Minnesota members thus got a unique chance to experience the work of the entire musical community. They received from national authorities some of that inspiration, so essential if intangible, that Donald Ferguson had espoused. The national president, William Arms Fisher, tackled the topic "What is Music?" and ended his wide-ranging philosophical and spiritual exploration with the words:

> We can understand why in music we find release, because we then transcend the narrow boundaries of self; for a brief space we break through its circumscribing fences, as music by its winged utterance carries us toward the portals of the great, all-inclusive Self.[24]

With these events MMTA realized that it was "here to stay" and celebrated by producing a Quarter-Century History written by the brilliant soprano, Jessica De Wolf. Heroes of the past, Gustavus Johnson, Clarance Marshall, and Emil Oberhoffer were given honorary memberships. Everything suggested a brilliant future. The first president of MMTA, Clarance Marshall, sent a letter from Texas full of confidence for the time to come.[25]

The newly-established recitals by local artists and the convention recitals by nationally-acclaimed artists were now joined by an exciting MMTA venture: a concert by student winners chosen in statewide competition. It began in the season of 1928–29 in a small way. The first year there were only 100 entrants, 97 from the Twin Cities, one from Detroit Lakes and two from Duluth, plus 25 entrants in a junior division, a part of the contest that was added only at the last moment.

To past and present officers and members
Minn. Music Teachers' Association -
    Greeting : -
        From the wide spaces, dim lines, isolated crotchets
of the Southwestern frontier, where musicians are still
toying with kinder-garten blocks and cutting paper dolls.
        Your idea of assembling past presidents is most excellent
and it is with deepest regret I post this letter instead of
purchasing a railroad ticket and partaking of the luncheon
which will surely be a feast - of reminiscenses
        I am proud that the infant organization I fathered a quarter
century ago has grown to voting age and has many future
years of "expectancy" - as insurance men express it.
May this future be long and happy.

        May your fingers have facility,
        Your fiddle bows virility,
        Your vocalists vivacity -
        Composers perspicacity.

        To M.T.A. longevity,
        With public receptivity
        For music of profundity
        And classical fecundity.

Fort Worth, Tex.
April 29 - 1928.

Marshall's letter

The music dealers of the Twin Cities provided prizes for the winners—
$100 for the First Piano Prize down to $7.50 in merchandise for the second-
place juniors. Though this contest was limited it none the less set in motion a
chain of events that was to lead over the years to an influential and widely-
supported contest involving thousands of students.

The senior winners of this first contest performed a lengthy and demanding program. Two of the senior performers, Harriet Johnson and Earl Rymer
were soon to be scholarship students of Olga Samaroff at the Juilliard
Graduate School—Johnson eventually became music critic of the *New York
Herald Tribune* and assistant to Samaroff in her Layman's Music Classes—

Rymer became a professor at the University of Minnesota and founder of a private music school.

Senior Program by Contest Winners
28 May 1929, Hotel Lowry, St. Paul

I. VIOLIN	Concerto in G Minor Prelude & Adagio Slavonic Dance in E Minor <div align="center">Dorothy Humphrey Mrs. J. Rudolph Peterson, piano</div>	Bruch Kreisler
II. VOICE	Tally Ho Spirit-Flower Jewel Song (Faust) <div align="center">Gertrude Schmitt Harriet Johnson, piano</div>	Leoni Campbell-Tipton Gounod
III. PIANO	Prelude and Fugue in G Minor Intermezzo in E Flat Etude in F Minor <div align="center">Eunice Ryan</div>	Bach Brahms Liszt
IV. CELLO	First Sonata, Opus 32 Meditation <div align="center">Betty Gillespie Edna Lou Smith, piano</div>	Saint-Saëns Gounod
V. VOICE	Dawn in the Desert Wild Geese (ms.) Voce di donna (La Gioconda) <div align="center">Frances DeVoice Miss Clara Williams, piano</div>	Ross Adams Ponchielli
VI. VIOLIN	Symphonie Espagnole Allegro non troppo Lotus Land Tambourin Chinois <div align="center">Beata Hanson Ethel Mae Bishop, piano</div>	Lalo Cyril Scott Kreisler
VII. PIANO	Etude in G Minor Mazurka in A Flat Prelude in F Major Ballade in A Flat <div align="center">Earl Rymer</div>	Chopin Chopin Chopin Chopin

Such a passing of the torch to younger musicians became one of the major achievements of MMTA. Encouragement offered at an early stage has frequently been paid back later in service to the association and to other youthful musicians. Rymer, for instance, became a contest judge, a consultant on teacher certification, and conductor of the Ten-Piano Ensembles of MMTA.

J. Victor Bergquist

How wonderful it would be if there were space to mention all those with similar early recognition and later contributions!

The music critics were delighted with the MMTA contest and the quality of its prize winners. In the public's mind, however, the first contest seemed relatively insignificant compared to the more prominent public school contests which began the same year: the State High School Music Contest[26] and the great Band Contest.[27] These could boast of casts of thousands and were announced in banner headlines that dwarfed MMTA's efforts—an ominous foreshadowing of the next decade when public school *educators* would seriously challenge MMTA *teachers*.

When Donald Ferguson became president in 1924, he secured a reinstatement of the examination method of certification. In addition, he launched a vigorous drive to secure public school credit for lessons given by accredited teachers of MMTA. His campaign was continued by J. Victor Bergquist,[28] organist and well-known composer of the First School of Minnesota Composition, who took over in 1927. Bergquist, a long-time leader of MMTA, occupied a unique spot because he served both the public sector as Assistant

Supervisor of Music in the Minneapolis schools and the private sector as a teacher at the MacPhail School. He knew the "music business" from direct experience in his various positions from private teacher right up to the directorship of the conservatory at Augustana College, Rock Island, Illinois.

Bergquist had witnessed the demise of the Illinois State Music Teachers Association,[29] and now he used every power he had to assure that Minnesota's association should remain in a healthy condition. He and his executive committee met each week and informed the 4,000 music teachers of the state of their actions through the *Northwest Musical Herald,* now the official organ of MMTA.[30] At the same time they wrote to every school superintendent, "urging upon them the plan" to give high school credit for private lessons.[31]

The time seemed ripe for government recognition of music students and teachers. Bergquist could dream of recitals "in the classrooms, the school auditoriums and the town halls," a possibility of placing the "music teacher on a par with the English teacher.[32] Donald Ferguson, the philosopher of the group could dream of music placed in the same lofty realm as the great classics of English writing.

> The literature of music is beyond the scope of preparatory courses. It is like the literature of English; so large and varied that no one person could begin to master it. But just therein lies its value—in that it is the product of a great collective effort; and to be ignorant of it is to be ignorant of one of the major efforts of humanity. Music *is* a literature; it *is* a vital expression of human impulse; and as such it is a vehicle for education and demands a position in the schools.[33]

6

A Workable Procedure. . .
Difficult to Formulate

"A workable procedure. . . difficult to formulate." With these words Donald Ferguson, MMTA President 1924–1927, posed the problem of how to blend work of the private music teacher with that of the public school music teacher. The balance betweeen these two approaches became the principal issue of the period of 1919–1929 and, despite good will on both sides, led to a parting of the ways.

In the earlier part of the century, music instruction in the public schools had centered upon the elementary grades and upon singing. Supervisors of Music developed programs and then oversaw the work of the classroom teacher. Many supervisors—active members of MMTA, officers, workshop guides, and leaders of the Minnesota group—saw no conflict between the private and public teacher. They had, naturally, certain specialized concerns relating to their classroom work and therefore joined in 1907 the newly-founded Music Supervisors National Conference but continued their affiliation with MMTA.

This situation changed as high school education become common after World War I. In Minnesota, 218 schools offered high school instruction at the beginning of the century. By 1915, this number had more than doubled. Enrollment increased spectacularily rising to some 12,000 students in 1900, 42,000 by 1915, and over 97,000 by 1930.[1] As high schools grew, so did music courses. Already-thriving orchestras were joined after 1919 by bands that multiplied rapidly as instrument manufacturers, music stores,[2] and music supervisors, acting in concert, set up a system of instrument acquisition, contests and concerts.

The question became, "Who shall teach the students, the public school teacher or the private teacher?" The United States Bureau of Education surveyed the schools of the nation in 1913 and asked the question, "Is applied music under outside teachers, as piano, voice, violin, etc., credited as school work toward graduation?" The answer was: "This, the most recent feature of practice in relation to high-school music, as it is one of the most progressive, has already gained considerable favor."[3]

In 1917, a committee on music of the same federal bureau—including Elsie Shawe, MMTA member and Supervisor of Music in the St. Paul Public Schools—reported:

> Although a number of high schools are now offering courses in applied music, that is, voice, piano, violin, and sometimes other instruments, on the same basis as the other subjects, the general adoption of this plan can not reasonably be expected for some time to come, if it ever becomes feasible. It is, therefore, recommended that study of voice, piano, organ, violin, or any orchestral instrument, under special teachers outside of school, when seriously undertaken and properly examined and certified, shall receive regular credit toward graduation.[4]

Within Minnesota the most influential and well-developed plan of public school music occurred in Minneapolis where it was instituted in 1912–1913[5] by MMTA members, Thaddeus P. Giddings[6] and Donald Ferguson. It established a system of requirements and grading of students who were allowed high school credit for private lessons with certified MMTA teachers. It had one unique proviso: the student must be simultaneously enrolled in Ferguson's harmony course in the Minneapolis High Schools. The object was to carry musical instruction beyond mere instrumental technique and into the realm of understanding, to give students the elements of musical language.

Ferguson joined the University of Minnesota Music Department staff in the academic year of 1913–1914 and soon found that he did not have time for the high school program. His position was taken by Gertrude Dobyns,[7] an MMTA teacher of renown, who was already combining theory and piano instruction in her private work. She led the high school harmony classes toward a final yearly project in original composition, "a system of musical evolution for children, which results have proved remarkable."[8]

Her place was taken when she left for volunteer war work in 1918 by J. Victor Bergquist, long-time MMTA member and another musician with an exceptional European background and a distinguished record of composition. He was appointed Assistant Supervisor of Music for the Minneapolis Public Schools as well as Organist-Director of Central Lutheran Church and teacher of organ, piano, and composition at the MacPhail School of Music. Before his death in 1935, he and other distinguished judges had examined

*Gertrude Dobyns (in front of the music) in a relaxed moment
with her piano class, c. 1912 (note the lone male).*

over 1,200 high-school student compositions and presented yearly programs
of the best works.

Bergquist's byword was *self-expression* by which he meant that a child
should learn music as he or she learns language:

> feeling his joyful way, like the infant to whom letters are unintelli-
> gible and grammar unsuspected, toward freedom of thought, fu-
> ture facility of utterance, fuller appreciation of the significance of
> his art and a deeper understanding of its immortal masterpieces.[9]

These younger composers appeared at the 1920 MMTA convention and confirmed the belief that wonders could be worked with the high school students.

Caprice		Winnifred Reichmuth
The Spider and the Fly		
	Played by the composer	
Violin—Bondage		Avner Rakov
	Played by the composer	
Impromptu		Fredrikka Fjelde
Elfin Dance		Stella Lucas
Prelude		Lorraine Anderson
	Played by the composers	
Songs—		
A Dirge		Celius Daugherty
The Waning Moon		
Laurel and Cypress		
	Sung by Miss Lora Lolsdorf	
	Composer at the piano	
Characteristic Pieces		Loleta Stout
The Frog		
The Cricket		
The Butterfly		
Vacation Days		Melva Block
The Cottage		
A Stroll in the Woods		
	Played by the composers	
Violin—		
Melody in G Minor		Margaret Wigham
Melody in G Major		Lucy Crittenden
	Played by Lucy Crittenden	
Number Thirteen		Harriet Levinson
Spinning Wheel		
Two Preludes		Gwendolyn Brewster
Awakening		Isabelle Zanger
Dreaming		
	Played by the composers	
Songs—		
Twilight		Grace Larusson
Roadways		
	Sung by Miss Luisdorf	
	Composer at the piano	
Carnival of the Dolls		Dorothy Bates
Puppets Dance		
Elaine		
Tin Soldiers' Parade		
The Tea Party		
	Played by the composer	

Many of these high school composers were set on a life-long pursuit of musical culture. A number became professionals: Winnifred Reichmuth, a teacher at the MacPhail School of Music who played concertos several times with the Minneapolis Symphony; Celius Dougherty, a pianist and song composer who accompanied world-renowned singers, and Margaret Wigham who was nationally known as a composer of teaching pieces.[10]

Such a project, crowned with success, offered unusual advantages to the student, the schools, the community, and to MMTA as well. The director of the Minneapolis Symphony, Henri Verbrugghen, judged these composition contests for six years and said that "there is not a similar enterprize in the world."

The Minneapolis plan also addressed the needs of the casual student who could be served by instrumental class lessons. Not long after Giddings took over his school position, one of the elementary principals requested a piano teacher within the school. As this was organized in 1915, Giddings placed it in charge of MMTA member, Wilma Anderson Gilman. Together they worked out a *Public School Class Method for the Piano* which contained simple pieces, folk music and a number of original compositions by MMTA member, Stanley Avery. The method brought students through elementary steps and readied them for more advanced work with private teachers. The classes were at first wildly popular but gradually diminished in enrollment. In 1935, 54 schools were offering classes and by 1940, 39 still continued.[11]

A similar arrangement was made for the study of orchestral instruments—especially the violin. This was placed under the supervision of member Ruth Anderson, Wilma Gilman's sister. It grew to giant proportions. By the beginning of 1927, over 5,000 students were playing in school orchestras, with 16 orchestras and 8 bands in the high schools—and some 53 grade school orchestras![12]

Minneapolis had evolved a system to be envied—and copied.[13] With this sterling example in mind, MMTA began its campaign for official recognition by the State Board of Education. The association set out to discover exactly what was being done within the high schools outside of Minneapolis. Toward this end, Bergquist sent a questionnaire to 625 schools. Along with his queries he sent a copy of the Minneapolis plan, the statement of the Minnesota State Board of Education that they had never ruled on the question, and the results of a national survey published by the National Bureau for the Advancement of Music.

Out of 350 Minnesota schools replying, 53 said they were giving credit for outside music study and 166 said they would like the services of MMTA.[14] Bergquist concluded that at least a significant number of schools were interested and that MMTA had a mission. Ferguson then sought and obtained the support of the MMTA plan by the Women's Clubs of the state. The time was ripe to approach the State Board of Education.

Armed with the success of Minneapolis, the certification program and the support of many in the community, MMTA confidently saw no reason why individual lessons should not carry high school credit. The Board of Education, however, generally did not concern itself with individual instruction. It dealt with students *en masse*. Furthermore, it was attempting, under the strict leadership of James M. McConnell, to set general regulations and to standardize what had become over the years a jerry-built system of schools. The Board had before it the example set by the music supervisors of the state who viewed the high school emphasis on large performing organizations, band, orchestra, choir—which the supervisors were developing brilliantly—as the proper outgrowth of the years of singing and general music in the grade schools.

At the meeting of 5 August 1924, the Board of Education considered a number of questions relating to high school graduation standards and decided that music and art should be counted toward high school graduation only when:[15]

> a. The subject is taught by a properly qualified and certified teacher of public school music or art employed by the school board.
> b. Due consideration is given to the effort and achievement of the pupil.
> c. The time element is on the same basis as for other school credits.

This seemingly closed the door on recognition of the MMTA plan. In essence, the Board refused to consider the association a faculty and therefore incapable of granting degrees or even accreditation.

Further confirmation of the Board of Education's view became public with the appearance of the state high school syllabus of 1925 which recognized music only in passing.[16] It was not listed either as a Constant or Non-Constant. Under the heading of "Worthy Use of Leisure," music got four words as a "common means of enjoyment."[17] For Allied Activities such as "debating, publications, subject clubs, bands and orchestras, athletic teams and student councils," the Board thought that granting of high school credit had— despite the example of Minneapolis that was attracting national attention— only "some slight vogue in scattered sections of the country." Their final opinion was: "it has been definitely discouraged in Minnesota . . . there may well be some phases of his activities in which a student will participate without such artificial rewards as marks and credit."[18]

In rejecting MMTA's request, the State Board of Education laid the groundwork for the complete separation of private *teachers* and public *educators*. MMTA's certification plan became a double-edged sword: it gave professional recognition to private teachers but it held little attraction for public high school teachers who more and more had both college degrees and state recognition. They therefore were little interested in taking further examinations or in MMTA itself.

There could hardly have been a bigger gulf between the attitude that relegated music to a "common means of enjoyment"—entertainment with perhaps a little value as "training"—and Bergquist's conviction that a child had the right to "self-expression in this univeral tongue" or Ferguson's credo that music was "one of the major efforts of humanity." The workable procedure, so long in preparation, had proved not only difficult to formulate but impossible to implement.[19]

A Century of Progress

in

American Music

AMERICAN INDIAN MUSIC

BIRTH OF OUR NATIONAL AIRS

FAMOUS CHARACTERS IN DEVELOPMENT OF MUSIC

> Lowell Mason (Stanley Avery)—Singing School (Members of Chorus from Minnesota School of Business—*Jack Sayres, President*)

STEPHEN FOSTER SONGS—Old Uncle Ned

Old Folks at Home

FIRESIDE TRIO—

> Miss Mildred Dahl
> Miss Elsa Larson
> Miss Anne Olsen
> (*Courtesy of J. Otto Jellison*)

"RAMPANT VIRTUOSI"

> (a) Jenny Lind - - - - - *Corrinne F. Bowen*
> (b) Ole Bull - - - - - *William MacPhail*
> (c) Sensational Pianist—Signora Pound-di-Keys - -
> - - - - - - - *Wilma Anderson Gilman*

SONGS OF THE CIVIL WAR

> Song of the North
> Song of the South
> Song of the Union
> Members of the Orpheus Club of St. Paul
> (*Courtesy of Malcolm McMillan, Director*)

POPULAR DANCE OF THIS PERIOD

> Virginia Reel (to the romantic strains of "Turkey in the Straw," played by the fiddlers, Francis Brewer and Cyril Schommer)

1933: The Opening Numbers of MMTA's Optimistic Program in Time of Stress

7

The Present Era of Enforced Leisure

The wry jest of "enforced leisure"[1] masked the dire conditions of the Thirties. About one in four working people was without income. Frequently the unemployed did not have even a penny in the household. In these circumstances they planted gardens, bartered for services, and sought help from more affluent relatives or, as a last resort, from charity. They did not dream of things that we might consider necessities—dental care, eye glasses, telephone—or the simple ability to "get away" from constant cares that pressed upon them day after day. In such circumstances, music became a luxury. How could one afford an instrument? How could one afford lessons? How could one afford a concert?

Many of the dreams of the Roaring Twenties vanished. Organists, pianists and stage bands were no longer needed as the Talkies replaced silent films. Nor were musicians necessary to local radio stations who drew their programs not from the community but from large national networks. It seemed to musicians that they had been hit twice, once by the economic disaster and again by the march of technology. In 1933, the depths of the depression, the American Society of Composers published a symposium, *The Murder of Music*, with the following statistics:[2]

Sale of pianos	$93,670,000	(1925)	$12,000,000	(1931)
Sale of phonographs	$46,000,000	(1927)	$4,869,000	(1931)
Royalties (records)	$780,568	(1927)	$86,000	(1932)
Sheet music	$3,447,775	(1926)	$827,154	(1932)
Movie orchestra members	19,000	(1926)	3,000	(1932)

Minnesota musicians were not spared. In Minneapolis, for instance, the new decade brought chaotic changes among the employed in its fifty theaters.[3]

Prior to the Talkies	After the Talkies
270 musicians (excluding organists)	82 orchestral musicians
$12,150 total weekly salaries	$3,690 total weekly salaries
30 organists	3–4 organists
$3,690 total weekly salaries	$200 total weekly salaries

Some prominent musical groups barely escaped dissolution. The pride of Minnesota, the Minneapolis Symphony, squeezed by in the 1932–33 season only by a near miracle.[4] Well-established schools had to adjust. St. Agatha's Conservatory, faced with plummeting enrollments, sent its teachers out into the regular parochial schools for satellite music lessons. Then after lunch and required prayers, the sisters "spent all afternoon and evening teaching students at the conservatory."[5]

Individuals had to find imaginative solutions to their everyday problems. MMTA member Madeleine Titus saved money while a student at the MacPhail School by walking something over four miles to get to her lessons and back. Later as she herself was a teacher, she commuted to Wisconsin and "exchanged overnight lodging with dinner (plus studio privileges) for piano lessons to her host family, a barter system pervasive in the thirties. Meager as it was, it worked exceedingly well."[6]

At first problems appeared temporary. "Prosperity is just around the corner" became the watchword. The cyclical nature of depressions was poorly understood. School textbooks on economics still reported solemnly on the connection between unusual sunspot activity and economic decline. People who could remember crises of the past believed that one or two years would be the duration.

More astute observers realized that this crash was to be prolonged. Well into the second year of the decade's "downturn," George Draper Dayton of Minneapolis told President Herbert Hoover that conditions were not improving and that the problems were spreading throughout the country.[7] Nation and state were not prepared for prolonged troubles. Charities were soon overwhelmed. Relief costs in Minnesota soared from "a negligible amount in 1929 to more than $9 million in 1933, and then to $33 million the following year."[8] In actuality, severe problems persisted right up to the start of World War II.[9]

The populace reacted to suffering and discouragement with remarkable vitality. Radio, movies and sports gave people relatively cheap entertainment and information. Humor similar to the jest in the title of this chapter continued in songs such as the brash "Who's Afraid of the Big Bad Wolf?" the quirky "The Music Goes Round and Round and it Comes Out Here," or the alluring "Lullaby of Broadway."

Music continued to thrive. Many homes had traditions of family singing. Church and social choirs were held in high esteem. Pianos were still common pieces of furniture. Many an evening ended with guests and hosts gathered around the piano singing "old favorites."

On the highest professional levels, Minnesota was blessed with two of the finest symphony conductors that could be found: Eugene Ormandy and Dimitri Mitropoulos. In choral music the St. Olaf College Choir was setting a new standard throughout the world. These established groups were joined by new ones sponsored by the WPA, the Works Project Administration, under the Federal Music Project: the Minnesota (WPA) Symphony Orchestra, Minnesota Symphonic Band, Twin Cities Dance Band, Jubilee Singers, Duluth Civic Band and the Virginia Dance Band. Their performances in schools, concerts and fairs brought music to a vast array of listeners previously unexposed to the art.

In the face of this crisis, MMTA redoubled its efforts to remain the strong organization it had become and to avoid the breakdowns that seemed to surround it. The Iowa Music Teachers Association under the "smothering" effect of the depression became dormant for the period of 1934–1945.[10] The Illinois group became inactive from the 1920s up until 1940. Indiana likewise faded during the years of 1923–1944.

First, MMTA instituted economies. Annual dues in the period 1925–29 had been $5.00, a just figure for the roaring twenties but quite a large figure in depression days. Now the fee was reduced to $3.00 and conventions were reduced to 2-day affairs rather than the usual 3-day offerings. With economies and depression came a loss of revenue. The budget had run at well over $1,000 per year. That was reduced to $600 to $700 at best. So difficult had the situation become that when the books for 1932 were balanced, only $2.87 was on hand and for 1933 this was reduced to $1.20. Examinations for certification had always been expensive. As another economy MMTA decided not to print examination questions but rely on mimeographed copies or even carbon copies. There is even some indication that they skimped on the certificates awarded to successful applicants.

Second, members determined not to react from fear and abandon their long-developing basic programs. Their certification process already had achieved a remarkable success. By the beginning of 1932, MMTA had awarded the following certificates:

Licentiate level	696 certificates
Associate level	81 certificates, comprising:

8 in organ
52 in piano
2 in public school music
9 in violin
10 in voice

The 696 Licentiate Certificates included 113 for sisters of the Catholic con-
gregations, yet another indication of how valued the MMTA program was
and, in addition, the impressive role that the sisters played in keeping music
alive during the depression.

With this success in attracting support for certification, MMTA tried once
again to get official recognition from the State Board of Education. Two
MMTA presidents of the period 1929–1934, Carl A. Jensen,[11] newly-
appointed director of the Macalester College Music Department and Harry
W. Ranks,[12] Coordinator of Applied Music in the Minneapolis Public Schools
fought valiantly for what they considered the next step.

They had the support of many members but were opposed by the active
member John Hinderer who with local, out-of-state speeches and nationally-
published articles stated forcefully his opposition. Hinderer was convinced
that any state regulation would be too drastic and not in accord with what he
considered to be the Jeffersonian ideal of democracy: "The less government
the better."[13] The issue, in the event, never reached the stage where MMTA
was forced to accept state rules. A drastic change of state board personnel—
and therefore opinion—occurred in 1934 and MMTA lost its bid for governmental licensing.

The question of who should receive state recognition was resolved in favor
of "educators," not "music teachers." Even before the depression, educators
had begun to organize. In 1924, the leaders of municipal and school bands
formed the Minnesota Bandmasters Association. As high school enrollments
increased dramatically so did the school band programs. In 1915, there had
been only one high school band—Mankato—but by 1921 five large cities and
one small one had begun programs. The roaring twenties was witnessing yet
another remarkable expansion. So rapid was the growth of bands that in
1928 the Bandmasters Association expressed its astonishment.

> The possibilities of the future are almost beyond imagination. But
> one thing is certain—we are on the eve of great accomplish-
> ments—the musical standards of America are due for a big up-
> lift—and it is all to be brought about through school music.[14]

The educator's optimism existed as well in their national organization, the
Music Supervisors National Conference, which in 1933–34 transformed itself into the Music Educators National Conference, MENC. The conference
maintained that one should convey the *love* of music rather than the traditional *technical* background of the art. The leader of the Flint [Michigan]
Community Music Association, William W. Norton,[15] a former Minnesotan,

Harry Ranks

Carl A. Jensen

asked the basic questions: "Are we truly *music educators*—or are we merely *teachers of music*?"

> Are we so absorbed in music, as such that we forget the children, or are we imbued with spiritual ideals that are sought through the experiences which we make available to the children? . . . Are we interested in education or are we merely interested in music? . . . Are we glorifying and perfecting the amateur ideal? Is the love of singing and playing carrying over into the community, into the church, the club, the neighborhood, the home?[16]

To create amateurs, that is, those who love music! What a noble ideal! Particularly so at the time of depression when the populace needed the arts as a means of envisaging a better world. The craving for inspiration was similar to the crisis of World War I when Community Sings brought people together to share in the drive for war and peace; now music of bands and orchestras united citizens and allieviated the heartache of the depression. There seemed to be a unique chance to "educate the public in an appreciation of musical opportunities" as the Federal Music Project put it.[17]

On the *teacher's* side, however, "merely interested in music" were fighting words. So they appeared to the president of the Chicago Musical College,

Glenn Dillard Gunn, who insisted that both educators and teachers should have one standard alone: "Music must be made with technical adequacy," something he found sometimes brilliantly achieved in the high schools and sometimes missing. Dunn recognized the basic dichotomy: "I want to make artists. You, by your own profession of faith, are dedicated to the training of amateurs. . . Your purpose is to develop a love of fine music; to do this in the only way it can be done—that is, through experience."[18]

In truth, both sides had validity. Some people who were students under the strict *teaching* regime of Giddings speak of the fear rather than the love he inspired. Students who aspired to professional music found that they had to take private lessons to fill the gaps left in the *music education* programs. We need both approaches. Although the two sides appear to have drawn up into opposing camps, they had to, and still have to, depend on each other as they develop lovers and masters of music.

8

How Greatly I Admire
Your Work and Aims

After the discouraging struggle for state recognition, it was a joy shortly after to find understanding and appreciation by one of the world's leading musicians. "How greatly I admire the work and aims you stand for" wrote Percy Grainger,[1] the noted pianist-composer, as he prepared to inaugurate a new program for MMTA. Even before this path-breaking event, MMTA had initiated yet another activity to make Grainger admire the group: a campaign to draw outstate teachers into the association's work. During the Depression, the association had lost its lines of communication. The Annual Reports and *Minnesota Music* had been dropped in 1921 and their successor, the *Northwest Musical Herald* had sputtered to a stop in 1934. The only solution, a self-help one typical of depression days, appeared to be the formation of stronger local and district units of MMTA.

President Harriet Allen,[2] elected for the 1934–1935 season and Wilma Anderson Gilman, State Chairman of Clinics, accepted the challenge. They started in Wadena on 15 April 1935. There they met local teachers in the Memorial Auditorium.[3] After a coffee hour to get acquainted, the two and Mr. Orville Trandson of the MacPhail School, played and discussed various musical pieces of the State Contest List. That afternoon, the Wadena group decided to build on the morning's start and voted to hold a number of clinics during the year with Miss Grace Bartlett as Local Chairman. In a new-found spirit of camraderie they finished the day with a dinner at the Commercial Hotel.

About 15 teachers from Detroit Lakes, Henning, Staples, Bertha, Long Prairie, Park Rapids, Sauk Center and Wadena attended this April meeting. By August the group was in full swing with a study of both piano and harmony requirements of MMTA, a lively talk on "How to Work with Pre-School Children" by Carolyn Bowen of the MacPhail School, papers on various aspects of teaching by the local members, solos by members and their

England.   Oct 27, 1936

Dear Mrs Gilman,
          Hearty thanks for your very
kind letter of Oct. 3, which I would have
had (& replied to) before had I not been
away in France with a sick friend.
          When I offered the Minneapolis program we
discussed together I was planning for seasons
in which I had many months a the year in USA.
But the last season & this coming one my time
in USA is very limited (3 – 4 months) so I promised
my manager to limit my concert activities for
these 2 seasons to <u>commercial concerts</u> (with
fees) only.   Hence her reply to your kind
proposal.   However, Mrs. Morse is very
sympathetic to my musical interests & she
knows how greatly I admire the work &
aims you stand for.   So I shall send
her a cable tomorrow morning, asking her
to accept less than $300 for me, if she feels
justified in doing so.
          Hoping something may come of your kind thot
& that I shall thus have the pleasure of
soon seeing you again,
                    Yrs heartily
                    Percy Grainger

Percy Grainger to Wilma Anderson Gilman

Harriet Allen

students, and exhibits of musical scores by the Paul A. Schmitt and Simon Music Companies.[4]

Shortly after launching this initiative, President Harriet Allen was taken sick and had to relinquish her position to Wilma Anderson Gilman,[5] an inspirational leader, who filled out Allen's term and was elected for the following year. She continued the outreach program even to the point of presenting a full-fledged district convention which was held at St. Cloud State Teachers College, 5 May 1936. A group of Minneapolis high school composers demonstrated what could be done with the study of music theory. John J. Becker, state director of music activities for the WPA, associate editor of *New Music Quarterly* and an outspoken advocate of the most advanced modern music, gave teachers his view of music's condition within the state.

The examples of Wadena and St. Cloud are indicative of a new life being infused into the various districts of the state. Now, in addition, Mrs. Gilman had a marvelous idea for the season of 1936–1937, a project that turned into the most far-reaching event—at least until the culminating syllabus program of 1970—in the history of MMTA. In her reminiscences, she described it thus:

> When I was president of the Minnesota Music Teachers Association, we were down to $68.00 in the treasury. I'd been to the music camp at Interlochen, Michigan, and I had seen Percy Grainger conduct twelve pianists with the band. I talked and bullied the executive board into setting up regional piano playing tryouts with ten-piano concerts in Minneapolis or St. Paul as a reward for the winners.[6]

The Executive Board did not think it would work. Interest, however, ran high and by October, Gilman could report that out-state applications had reached 125 entries for the first time. Wadena, for instance, held its first district contest with 12 students receiving a rating of "A." Three of these played in the first Massed Piano Concert in Minneapolis.

Everything seemed set for a winning convention on the 29th and 30th of December 1936 It was marred only by a typical Minnesota event. The *Minneapolis Star* reported:

> Minneapolis skidded and tumbled today after an all-night drizzle and slightly below freezing temperatures turned the city's streets and sidewalks into ice-glazed surfaces making both walking and driving extremely hazardous. Sleet covered a large section of the state, while a heavy fall of snow at St. Cloud, Willmar and Morris added to the treachery of automobile travel.[7]

Wilma Anderson Gilman
(from a newspaper clipping)

GRAINGER
Pianist ⌢ Composer

In Recital and Directing
TEN MASSED PIANOS

•

LYCEUM THEATER
December 30th, 8:15 P. M.

•

Popular Prices: 25c—$1.00

•

AUSPICES MINNESOTA MUSIC TEACHERS ASS'N

Mgr. ANTONIA MORSE, White Plains, N. Y.

Cover page of the Grainger concert

Despite the storm, the Ten Massed Pianos were assembled at the Lyceum Theater, Percy Grainger arrived and the winning students performed the following program.

Program

I. THE GUITAR   *Gaynor-Carter*
    MINUET (Sonata Op. 45, No. 2)   *Beethoven-Frothingham*
    SICILIENNE   *Bach-Maier*
        Gail Storlie   Jane Allen
        Vernon Mark   Miles Labovitch
        June Engen   Bernard Lindgren
        Irene Berde   Jack Hayes
        Marjory Youngquist   Sylvia Taylor
            (Ages 10–12 years)

II. MUSETTE   *Bach-Kosakoff*
        Marilyn Dewass   Patricia Hayes
        Lois Elaine Kaplan   Phyllis Lund
            (Ages 6–9 years)

III. WHITE JASMINE   *Dungan*
     TWO MUSICAL RELICS OF MY MOTHER   *Grainger*
     BLITHE BELLS   *Bach-Grainger*
     ANDANTE & SCHERZO   *Mozart-Maxim*
        Phyllis Lightfield   Helen Kessler
        Joan Adelle Johnson   Adah Packerman
        Doreen Conner   Dennis Andal
        Elizabeth Abeler   La Verne Bjorklund
        Ronald Gearman   Paul King
            (Ages 13–16 years)

IV. FUGUE IN A MINOR   *Bach-Grainger*
    VALSE VIENNOIS   *Parrish*
    CHILDREN'S MARCH   *Grainger*
        Jane Axness   Jean Anderson
        Maxine Ingmundson   Isabelle Behrend
        Harriet Morin   Lenore Engdahl
        Margery Gregory   Josephine Wetteland
        Joyce Westrom   Viola Mathowetz
                Assisted in the Fugue by
        Evelyn Distad   Marian Chapman
        Lucella Hartwell   Ann Darby
        Judith Ann Williams   Estelle Larsen
        Virginia McCloud   Richard Hanson
        Kathryn Thorpe   Richard Clausen
            (Ages 17–21 years)

The evening came to a glorious finale when Grainger played four solos.

Intermezzo, E flat, Op. 117, No. 1	*Brahms*
Rhapsody, G minor, Op. 79, No. 2	*Brahms*
Pagodas	*Debussy*
(based on Javanese Gamelan music)	
"Islamey" Oriental Phantasy	*Balakeriew*
(based on Tartar themes)	

Gilman considered the first concert to be a flop. She, however, judged solely from the financial angle. From the pedagogical viewpoint it was a stunning success. Students were thrilled to be able to play under the direction of a master musician so well-known to Minnesota.[8] The concert even proved a revelation to some. Leonore Engdahl, one of the performers, many years later, described her awakening to the music of Bach in a letter to then-president, Russell Harris.

> The day before your letter reached me I had described, to a student, my exciting introduction to J. S. Bach. It was *that* concert and its preparation which unfolded the glorious music to me. I do not recall which voice of the *A-minor Fugue* (Well Tempered Clavier Vol. I) I studied. But when our group met for its first rehearsal, and all the voices joined, I experienced what is known today as a "mind blowing" excitement and rapture.[9]

By the second season of Ten Massed Pianos, Mrs. Gilman's hopes for a financial success were fulfilled. A number of music firms were willing to provide pianos. St. Catherine's College and the University of Minnesota began to provide concert halls. The 35¢ fee that each member of the public paid covered expenses with some extra left over.

Each year thereafter the association added some special attraction which would prove appealing to the parents and the public.

1937	An ensemble of 20 violin winners and the Hamline A Cappella Choir
1938	Minneapolis A Cappella Choir and South High School Band
1939	Violin and Cello Solos, Piano Ensemble of MMTA Teachers
1940	St. Mary's Orthodox Choir
1941	Bach Ensemble Concerto with small orchestra

Chester Campbell

In 1937 and 1938, a brief interest in violin was spurred by the election of Chester Campbell,[10] one of four presidents who played that instrument, but by 1942, it became clear that piano ensembles could fill the entire evening although a few vocal or instrumental solos were included to give variety.

After the first few years, the organizers found that certain extremely talented students would win consistently so MMTA instituted a practice of requiring those students to move up an age bracket. Such special students were identified by asterisks beside their names—a system allowing for "stars" without in any way detracting from the "winners" who each received a special certificate signed by the president of MMTA. Many of these documents still reside among treasured family heirlooms.

The grand finale of the year compensated for the day-by-day, often lonely, hours of practice. Students could meet other aspirants of their own ages, new friends within the musical community. Parents now could now bask in state recognition of the art of music and their children's accomplishments. Family sacrifices of time and money had not been in vain. Teachers found that more and more students wanted to study as they saw that rewards did not go solely to one or two students but to larger groups. Here indeed was that "radiating" of music that Charles Henry Mills had postulated at the 1912 MMTA convention. Despite the Great Depression and the impending war clouds of Europe, MMTA had found a focus. The association had trapped that rare animal: an event as helpful to themselves as to the community.

Agnes Rast Snyder

As the new initiatives gathered momentum, Agnes Rast Snyder,[11] who had served as Program Chairman, seemed the natural choice for president. She was elected for the convention of 1939 and served the longest continuous term of any president—from 1939 through the convention of 1945. For the 1940 season, she arranged a primary convention at Duluth followed in the fall by a second convention in Minneapolis. As crown to this expanded out-reach program and as a celebration of MMTA's fortieth year, she invited the MTNA to hold its 1941 convention in Minneapolis. Carlyle Scott, now a na-tional vice-president, organized the meeting. Every important musical organ-ization of the state from the Hamline University Choir to the Minneapolis Symphony lent support.

The national delegates convened from 26 to 31 December 1941 with the theme "American Unity Through Music." The coverage was broad.[12] Papers ranged from scholarly reports on the sixteenth-century chanson to practical matters of violin technique—but time and again sessions returned to the American theme. The convention opened with a piano recital by John Kirkpatrick, the noted exponent of contemporary United States music.

PROGRAM

I.	Sonata (1928–30)	*Roger Sessions (1896–)*
	Andante—allegro—	
	andante—poco meno mosso—	
	andante—molto vivace	
II.	Three Preludes (1941)	*Robert Palmer (1915–)*
	Vivace	
	Molto tranquillo	
	Allegro con energia	
III.	Sonata (1934–36)	*Hunter Johnson (1906–)*
	Allegro molto e dinamico—	
	andante—	
	scherzo e coda	

IV.	Fantasy	*Ross Lee Finney (1906–)*
V.	Capriccio (1940)	
	Toccata (1939)	*Theodore Chanler (1902–)*
	Evocation No. 1 (1937)	*Carl Ruggles (1876–)*
	Pawnee Horses (Omaha melody) (1905)	
	Navajo War Dance No. 2 (1908)	*Arthur Farwell (1872–)*

Other major concerts brought the WPA Orchestra with compositions of Robert Ward, Ross Lee Finney, Burrill Phillips and more; and the Minneapolis Symphony with songs by Donald Ferguson and a symphony by Howard Hanson. Unprecedented riches came to members of MMTA who flocked to the convention—368 Minnesotans out of 744 in attendance.

Among the triumphs for the state was Donald Ferguson's presentation "What is a Musical Idea," an exposition of how music could convey a definite emotional message in addition to its sonic and formal qualities. "Fergie," as he was affectionately known, had ideas which had inspired the Minnesota group on several occasions. Now the national delegates, electrified by his exposition, gave him a standing ovation.

The newly-declared war against Japan, Italy and Germany hovered over this 1941 convention. In the years immediately following, under the restraints on travel, the national group was not able to mount another full convention until the year 1946.[13] The Minnesota group, so beautifully poised for expansion, had to abandon its outreach program although yearly conventions and the 10-piano event continued in Minnesota—patronized almost exclusively by teachers in the Twin Cities. During the war years, only 4 or 5 teachers a year from outstate were able to send students to the prestigious piano programs.

The wartime crisis coincided with a musical one: the turn toward what was called "modern music." This style had taken root in the 1920s when the League of American Composers began to commission and perform modern works in New York City and began to publicize their work through the journal *Modern Music*. Adding to the work of the league, in the 1930s, WPA musical groups took up the crusade.

In Minnesota, a particularly forceful impetus came from Dimitri Mitropoulos, conductor of the Minneapolis Symphony. His audience, unaccustomed to the new musical language, deserted him on occasion. One-third or more of the listeners left the hall during a particularly extreme work—only to return for the next concert because he gave all of his effort and perceptive feeling to each work, traditional or avant garde.

The modern movement gained still more energy when Ernst Krenek, Viennese composer, became head of the music department of Hamline University in St. Paul. He soon joined forces with Mitropoulos, and other like-minded members of the musical community: Louis Krasner, concertmaster of the Minneapolis Symphony, and James Aliferis, choral conductor of the University of Minnesota.[14]

Soon a local chapter of the International Society for Contemporary Music came into being. Concerts of that society and of various colleges attracted small but devoted audiences. Few people who attended will forget the performances in Bridgeman Hall at Hamline University or the visiting stars of the new movement such as John Kirkpatrick playing the Concord Sonata of Ives or Henry Cowell demonstrating tone-clusters.

MMTA, well aware of the necessity of keeping abreast of stylistic developments, began to feature "modern" music at its conventions. Names like Prokofiev, Bartók, Shostakovitch, Honegger, Milhaud, Hindemith, Copland, and Ruggles began to appear on MMTA convention programs. Krenek spoke to members on "A Composer Teaching," Helen Greims demonstrated "Contemporary Piano Music for the Intermediate Student," and Krasner and Krenek performed a sonata by Martinu.

The real question for MMTA was how the new style could be transmitted to the larger membership. Many experienced music teachers—and even devoted concert-goers—were shocked by the degree of "dissonance" in the new works. They heard "discord," not brighter color. First-hand experience with the new pieces became essential. MMTA responded. Each year a committee

Robert N. Pearson

of veteran teacher-musicians drew up a carefully balanced list of compositions at the various age levels. Special attention was given to providing examples drawn from the various stylistic periods: baroque, classic, romantic, impressionist, and modern. Soon compositions by Prokofiev, Krenek, Griffes, Creston, Bartók, Kabalevsky and others on the contest lists began to tempt teachers to expand their repertories and their libraries.

Despite the exhilaration of the massed piano concerts, the emergence of an exciting new musical style and the resiliance that allowed MMTA to survive the war years, the organization had lost a great deal of ground. In 1946, only 259 students registered[15] for the contest—not an impressive number at all if we remember that the first contest in 1929 attracted 125. Just as depressing were the other statistics. In 1948, MMTA had only 177 members—not significantly above the figure established back in 1902 at the first full convention. Above all, the teacher certification program had gradually dwindled away. The last entry for embossing of a Licentiate Certificate seems to date from 1948 though the Examining Board, responsible for the testing program, is listed for two more years and then dropped.

Devoted members of this depleted group soon began a rebuilding program. Presidents Carl A. Jensen and Robert N. Pearson[16] developed a new constitution. Changes were more or less administrative: three vice-presidents took over the duties of treasurer, membership and contest chairman. More than cosmetic changes were needed. It was time for a revival of basic ideals which had been fostered for almost a half-century—but a revival that incorporated the new with the old.

⚭

Paul M. Oberg

9

We are Growing

At this crisis point, MMTA found a leader well acquainted with the history of MMTA. Dr. Paul Oberg,[1] newly-appointed Chairman of the Departments of Music and Music Education of the University of Minnesota, had benefited from the Minneapolis High School System of music theory and original composition. In college during the roaring twenties, he had been a student of Donald Ferguson, president of MMTA . Now in 1948, he could bring a wide experience in music making: piano and organ performance, musicological studies, years of college teaching, and a desire to foster contemporary composition.

Oberg approached his presidential position full of energy. In his first year with MMTA, he moved the Ten-Piano Concerts to the large prestigious space of Northrop Memorial Auditorium, home of the Minneapolis Symphony. Soon he began to restore the outreach program, first, with mid-winter meetings held in the Twin Cities, and then, by workshops in outstate districts. Eventually during his presidency sixty-eight new members were added to the rolls.

In these same years, he scoured the nation to find enterprising replacements for his older university faculty now at retirement age. Many of these new voices became leaders and even presidents of an invigorated MMTA.

So pleased was the group that Oberg was elected for a year beyond the customary two. As he prepared to chair his third convention, his wife, Marcella, jokingly told him that if he were elected to a fourth term, he needn't bother coming home. When he was duly chosen, a goodly number of members rose to offer their homes to him. We can report that he returned happily to his own home where his wife shared with him his hopes and achievements for Minnesota—but also some concern for his heavy work schedule.

Oberg had arrived on the scene at a propitious moment. As John Thut said as he looked back on those years, "We are growing." No high-flown statement

John Thut

that. Just plain Minnesota talk. The day of exalted pronouncements had passed; everyone was now busy trying to make up for the lost years of the war.

The country was coming out of the doldrums of both the Great Depression and of World War II. A recession had been averted. The GI Bill of Rights gave veterans an unprecedented opportunity for training and a smooth transition into the civilian economy. Many discharged soldiers found that they were able to achieve an education and a living far beyond their pre-war dreams. Colleges, vocational schools, conservatories were crowded with mature, earnest workers eager to begin careers.

The people on the home front had amassed savings during the time when goods were scarce. Now they could use that accumulation for houses and new products. Many began their after-war lives in suburbia, removed from the country farm life or the crowded city life of depression days. Prosperity reigned.[2]

The returnees came back as the joke had it, "to make babies." Elementary schools soon were flooded. The census figures for young Minnesotans tell the story better than any wordy explanations.

Children and Teens on the Minnesota Census

	1940	1950	1960	1970
Under 5 yrs	230,057	332,460	416,005	331,771
Ages 5–9	220,176	267,652	380,650	402,635
Ages 10–14	238,918	223,787	324,710	415,021
Ages 15–19	257,349	207,460	251,352	373,405

The demand for music lessons grew with the burgeoning population, a rise reflected in the 10-piano contest and concert.

1948	259 entrants	144 finalists
1958	1,350 entrants	497 finalists
1968	2,644 entrants	1,095 finalists

By 1970, it became necessary to expand the concert to twelve pianos—and within six more years to twenty pianos, double the ten that Percy Grainger had started with in 1935. Quality rose in a comparable fashion so that, in 1958, MMTA decided that the "Ten–Piano Concert" would be more accurately called the "State Honor Student Concert" or "Honors Concert."

A heroic effort went into each yearly program. The contest material had to be selected and published:[3] a list of six to nine compositions for each of seven age groups. Special care went into the selection of pieces for the Primary Group, students of 8 years of age and younger. Their tiny hands and beginning status dictated simple pieces which had at the same time to be attractive such as the following:[4]

Dandrieu	Menuet
Dandrieu	Quadrille
Frackenpohl	A Walking Tune
Henri Noel	One by One, Two by Two
Ernst Bacon	Melodious Sonnet
Colin Taylor	Pixie in the Wood

As students grew older, they were presented with a list of compositions in various styles from the Baroque to the Modern such as the following for Junior B, ages 11 and 12.[5]

Scarlatti	Sonata G Major, Longo 84
Rameau	Rigaudon
Haydn	Scherzo & German Dance
Mozart	Scherzo, Sonatine B-flat

Grieg	(1) Cowherd's Song &
	(2) Schubert's Waltz Op. 9A/1
Raphling	Jazz Toccata
Reizenstein	Exciting Story
Heller	Prelude Op. 119/32

Finally the Senior B students, ages 19 and 20, were expected to present moderate-length compositions of the standard concert repertory.[6]

Bach	First mvt., Italian Concerto
Haydn	First mvt., Sonata In E-flat,
C.P.E.Bach	Prussian Sonata 6,
	1st & 2nd mvts.
Chopin	Preludes Op. 45 and Op. 28/16
Brahms	Intermezzo E-flat minor, Op. 118/6
Debussy	Reflets dans l'eau
Griffes	Scherzo, Fantasy Pieces, Op. 6
Copland	Passacaglia

Many of the same criteria had to be applied to the development of the concert program itself. Most of this material was from original and transcribed piano-duet or two-piano literature. Usually the very youngest performers were placed early in the program while the seniors finished the concert with display numbers. The 1965 program given opposite was especially imaginative and shows the care taken for programming.

Primary (8 and under)
Song of the River   Last
The Sad Little Spinner   Barlow
Carnival Time   Scher

Junior A (9–10)
Sarabande   Cumming
Hungarian Folk Suite   Bartók-Suchoff
   Allegramente
   Adagio
   Molto Vivace

Junior B (11–12)
Wake Up (Sassafras)   Bacon-Gould
Garry Owen (Sassafras)   Bacon-Gould
Sassafras (Sassafras)   Bacon-Gould
Serenade No. 8   Persichetti

Intermediate A (13–14)
Marcietta and Berceuse   Casella
Cantina (Cafe Society)   Mundy
Noël d'Enfant   Respighi

Intermediate B (15–16)
Concerto for Two Pianos   Wigham
   Spirito
   Andante
   Allegro

Senior A (17–18)
Sonata Op. 87   Toch
   Allegretto
   Andante espessivo
   Allegretto amabile

Senior B
Russian Dance (Petrouchka)   Stravinsky

1965 State Honor Student Concert

Contest Day

Students waiting their turns

Once all of this work was finished and the list published each fall, individual teachers could decide which of their students might profit by the contest and what composition fitted that person's level of accomplishment.

While the teacher and student were learning, the Contest Chairman was busy arranging testing sites around the state, finding judges for each age group, distributing entry forms and receiving entry fees—for a mere 2,500 students! Or more! On an appointed Saturday in February, students and parents began arriving at colleges around the state. Each aspirant sat in a hallway waiting for his or her number to be called. Each judge listened intently for accuracy, technique, tone, and that elusive article called "style."

Finally all of the paper work came flooding back to the Contest Chairman who began all over again to register the high-scorers who progressed to the Final. In March, the successful students came to the Twin Cities for yet another round where the winners for the Honors Concert were chosen.

Gladys Markley

The field had by this time been narrowed to around 600 and the Contest Chairman could settle into making reports, preparing to send out certificates to winners, making the lists of winners and their teachers for the concert programs. . . and recuperating. Gladys Markley,[7] chairman for 17 years, told us in her quiet manner that her husband helped to sort entries and her children learned to alphabetize with the contest forms. She never mentioned that she was teaching a full class of students herself.

While Mrs. Markley's devotion surely was exceptional yet many teachers then—and now—went far beyond the call of duty. If there were space, we would like to chronicle their achievements. It would be simple justice to tell of each and every one of the legion of members who, as Bernard Shaw said of the civilized man, put more back into the common pot than he took out. We must, however, let one person's accomplishments stand for many.

At this point, the Concert/Rehearsal Chairman, assured that the winners were studying the concert numbers, began the great spring activity of finding space and rehearsal times for a mere 20 pianos. In the early years, such a huge affair required the services of several music companies,[8] but as time went on, the Schmitt Music Company, assumed the task of providing 20 well-tuned pianos in their warehouse rooms for rehearsal and finally on Northrop Auditorium stage for the concert.

Parents brought their children from all over the state to perform on a stage large enough for opera. Parents and friends found their places in the 5,000 seat auditorium. The tuner had worked over the pianos, and the State Contest Chairman and the Concert/Rehearsal Chairman and their host of volunteers—generally classified as ushers—had *only* the task of marshalling 600 students

Phillip Brunelle

At the Honors Concert

in their springtime finery, ages 6, 7 or 8 to 20 into formations to enter the stage.

As one group acknowledged their applause and exited, the next one marched to assigned pianos awaiting the conductor's signal to sit down. As they found their places on the piano benches, they looked up at the baton. The 6–8 years olds were dwarfed by the grand pianos. Conductor Philip Brunelle once announced to the audience that they probably could not even see the tots—but he could. That was what mattered. Rapport had been established with the conductor during the rehearsals and the performances went smoothly.

By the end of the evening, twenty to thirty groups had appeared. The audience had heard everything from little dances and character pieces to movements of sonatas and duo-piano pieces. MMTA teachers retired to homes and hotel rooms to rest so they might be bright and cheerful for next two days, the state convention.

To describe the annual contest/concert with the words "heroic effort" or Gladys Markley's "immensity of this project" may appear extreme. After the preceding explanation, the reader can readily understand that they are not an exaggeration. Almost every MMTA member was involved in some way; still, we must give special credit to the contest chairmen who bore the heaviest load.

1951–52	Dora Gosso
1953	Louise Cobley
1954, 1956	Barbara Wetzel Smith
1955, 1957–58	Margaret P. Berg
1959–1975	Gladys F. Markley

Each "Honor Concert" included a small number of advanced student winners, "Young Artists" who played solos at the ensemble concerts. Given the opportunity of good teaching and competition with their peers, enough students were achieving such excellence that a separate Young Artist Recital had to be instituted in 1966. From that point on, this recital became a feature of each yearly convention.

John Thut's understated words, "We are growing," masked a phenomenon. With the torrent of new students, membership in MMTA rose steadily.

1948	177 members
1958	301 members
1968	425 members

Teachers, spurred by eager youths and the possibility of doing truly professional work, recognized the need for increased quality in their own work. MMTA became more closely allied with national units. Presidents Dora Gosso[9] and Russell Harris[10] both made alliances with national and regional groups.

Harris, as president of the East Central Division of MTNA, planned and presided over a convention so large as to be truly on the scale of a national meeting.[11] In Minneapolis, 16–19 February 1958, delegates of Illinois, Indiana, North Dakota, Michigan, Minnesota, Ohio and Wisconsin joined with the American String Teachers Association for a great musical gala. The convention was built around the theme of "Ensembles"—the Augsburg College Choir, the Hamline University A Cappella Choir the University of

Dora M. Gosso

Russell G. Harris

Minnesota Chamber Singers and Massed Choir, the Eastman String Quartet and others. Minnesota won extraordinary approval and Harris, after twenty years of membership in MTNA, was launched on a thirty-year period of service to MMTA. The "radiating" of musical training so long desired by state and national associations was becoming more and more a living reality.

Despite all this activity, despite all the energy, Minnesota leaders realized that there were aspects of music that were not covered by the contest/concert. Students should be able to sight read scores, they should have a knowledge of music theory, they should be composing music. These became the goals of Oberg and the post-war presidents.

Oberg knew the value of theory training, particularly, the ability of students to truly "use" theory and not just file random facts in a back corner of the mind to be trotted out on state occasions.[12] He wrote to Henry Woodward, head of the Music Department of Carleton College, proposing a regional workshop:

> "We are striving to point out to applied music teachers the ne-
> cessity for making theory more practical. As you possibly know,
> a large number of our members have not had too extensive the-
> ory training, and we feel that an educational venture such as this,
> should be helpful to them."

One of his university appointees, Earl George, a brilliant young composer, convened in 1953 a group of college theory and composition teachers in an attempt to organize a special theory section within MMTA.[13] Unfortunately George left the state soon after and before official action could be taken by the association.

In 1955 Guy Duckworth arrived in the Music Department of the University of Minnesota. He soon took a leading role in MMTA: first as a panelist for the 1956 convention and then as the head of the materials committee and conductor of the Ten-Piano Concerts of 1957 and 1958. He was a strong advocate of group teaching and of students improvising and discovering—through listening—how music is composed—in short, music theory as a tool.

A group of his students performed for the 1961 MTNA Convention in Philadelphia.

> Convention delegates were enthralled with the four 10-year olds
> Duckworth brought with him. One of the numbers performed by
> the group was Henry Cowell's "Irishman Dances." It seems that
> Cowell was in the audience, and came up afterward to congratu-
> late the children on the performance.

One child asked Cowell if he would like him to play something
else using Cowell's tools. "What are my 'tools'?" Cowell asked.

"Tone clusters, open fifths, and D minor," the boy replied. He
then proceeded to play "Old Folks at Home"—Cowell style.[14]

Quite a few members observed Duckworth's methods or attended one of his
seminars. One of these, Louise Guhl, expressed what many discovered: "For
the first time in my life, I was playing by ear, transposing, and improvising . . .
always done with specified 'tools,' i.e. the musical structure of the material at
hand."[15]

Duckworth was far from the only person using theory as a tool. Many
members of the association were either using commercially–prepared theory
papers or were developing their own programs. Donald Anderson,[16] for instance, had each student write music. His daughter, the composer, Carol
Barnett, reports that "he would give them little snatches of poetry and they'd
set those [to music] and also theoretical concepts and they'd compose an example of what was this and what was that."[17] Other teachers were working
in similar ways. The time was ripe for the association to work out a course in
musical theory and a testing program to validate the student's work.

In 1962, President Robert Laudon[18] of St. Cloud State College invited
Louise Guhl[19] and her husband to dinner at his home. There, he presented the
theory situation—as well as a meal. Subsequently at the mid-winter meeting
in January of 1963, Guhl reported on several ways of improving the spring
contest including a proposal that an "optional theory test be set up at the
state level" and that consideration be given to "a creative work contest."

This met with approval and a theory committee consisting of Russell
Harris [Chairman], Justine O'Connor, Gordon Howell, Robert Laudon, June
Arnold, and Madeleine Titus soon began meeting to work out details of a
Level I test. Harris was a composer, O'Connor and Titus had been strongly
influenced by Duckworth, the others had actively fostered theory instruction
in their piano teaching. So committed were these individuals that they continued to meet regularly for several years even under adversity. One late
spring day after a heavy storm, they all made their way to Justine O'Connor's
studio by dodging around fallen trees, backing out of blocked streets, and
finding bizarre routes. Some members even brought items from their freezers
to store at Justine's home until power was restored to their part of the city.

When the committee submitted its first test at the elementary level,
MMTA members were hesitant. Each teacher realized how difficult it was to
pack information into a short lesson. Gradually, however, most found con-
structive ways of working and realized that theory instruction was helpful
enough to actually make lesson-time more effective.

Robert T. Laudon and contestant, Alice Threlkeld
Contest of 1971

Theory testing commenced in February of 1965. In 1966, 280 students were tested, by 1968 this had increased to 615. By 1969, tests were given in Levels I–IV and in 1970, 1,352 students were examined in five levels. This program imposed yet more burdens on the state contest—and the contest chairman who handled it in the early years—still it proved its worth and became a standard procedure from this point until the present day.

Simultaneously with these efforts to help the student, MMTA began to consider what association policies might help the teacher who needed security and respect. Some new procedure had to replace the older, now defunct, certification process.[20]

In his terms, 1963–1965, President Schuessler,[21] well-known vocal teacher and later head of the Music Department of the University of Minnesota, together with his board discussed ways of improving the image of the private teacher. They were aware of the Canadian system of music syllabi—a systematized means of guiding and assessing student work—under the control

Roy A. Schuessler

primarily of the University of Toronto and to a lesser extent the University of Manitoba. The MMTA board even had private discussions about the adoption of such a plan but because of other pressing problems the matter never became known to the membership.

In these post-war years, three classes of music teachers existed: those who had earned the bachelor's degree in music, those that had studied beyond that fundamental degree, and those that had no degree. It was true that more and more people were attending college and their degrees became certificates of musical background and teaching competency. Yet many of the older teachers, competent and skillful, did not have degrees. They might have studied privately with excellent masters and they frequently had years of solid teaching experience. Some compromise would be necessary. Music was a special case.

A committee under the chairmanship of Oberg, and with members, John Hinderer, Earl Rymer, Marie Holland Smith and William MacPhail Jr.[22] began to examine possible new plans of certification that would take account of emerging and traditional standards. When Anthony Chiuminatto[23] of St. Thomas College, a tireless crusader for accreditation, became president for the terms of 1965– 1967, he insisted, cajoled, explained, joked, and led members toward a new way of classifying teachers. He knew music teaching both in Europe and in the United States. He appreciated the high value given to music and teaching in Italy where a student entering the conservatory each day greeted the statue of Verdi with a "Bon giorno, maestro." He knew that in some countries, the students still stood when the teacher entered the room. Still, he also was keenly aware that these ways would never fit the more informal American scene.

Chiuminatto believed in certification by college degrees but he also realized that some sort of equivalency was necessary—at least in the formative stages of accreditation. There had to be equivalents of degrees. The matter finally came to a vote at the state convention chaired by John Thut of Augsburg College in of June of 1961.[24] Three levels were established: I: Graduate Accredited, II: Accredited, and III: Associate. It was agreed that all of the current membership as of 1960 would be certified at least at the Accredited grade.

Teachers were to be judged through an affidavit of their training and experience which would be evaluated by a committee of 1) Earl Rymer, University of Minnesota piano professor and the winner of the first MMTA contest in 1929, 2) Tony Chiuminatto, Chairman of the Music Department of St. Thomas College, and 3) Martha Baker, distinguished teacher of piano and eurhythmics at the MacPhail School and College of Music. This committee inspired confidence and worked diligently to expedite the enterprise. In such a delicate subject as this, understandably some hard feelings developed about the matter of "equivalency" but by 1962, notarized documents began pouring in. From that point on, MMTA has maintained, with periodic modifications, a type of certification derived from this scheme.

Still other steps transformed MMTA into a truly professional organization. Tony Chiuminatto prepared the first directory of the association and began to circulate an occasional newsletter. Russell Harris began a closer

Anthony L. Chiuminatto

association with the national and regional music teachers. John Thut made arrangements to have Mutual of Omaha issue medical insurance for the members of MMTA. Robert Laudon gained approval for affiliation with the State Organization Services, SOS, which handled the business of groups such as the nurses of the state. This gave MMTA a central office where correspondence and telephone calls could be directed and relieved the elected officers of much of the "busy-work" of an organization that was growing beyond the bounds of volunteer help.

By 1962, MMTA had become the envy of neighboring states. When the presidents of the East Central Region of MTNA met, they marveled at Minnesota's healthy financial balance of $8,000. The closest competitor was

Michigan which could muster $3,000. One state had only seventy-five cents on hand! No other state had an honor's concert, active district workshops, or an insurance plan. MMTA was even making an annual contribution to the funds of the Minneapolis Symphony. Minnesota held its own in membership as well: 333 members compared to 390 for Michigan and 319 for Illinois.

The association had entered the larger music sphere. The modern style was gradually being accepted and used, most particularly in the yearly contest repertory—although this required constant encouragement. As Chiuminatto said:

> The student who never reaches beyond the 19th-century com-
> posers is, musically, living in the past. As teachers of the young
> we have the moral obligation to keep them apace of their time
> with perception and discernment.[25]

He quoted Aaron Copland's scorn for those who "use music as a couch" whereas "contemporary music is meant to wake you up, not put you to sleep."[26]

As MMTA approached 1968, despite remarkable progress there remained issues which needed further attention. Only a tentative program for testing of sight reading had been attempted and it remained cumbersome and unworkable. Little had been done to encourage composition. No organized standardized program for students had been established.

Many obstacles stood in the way of any new program. Teacher accreditation continued to be a nagging question. Finances did not seem adequate for fresh ventures. Most crucial of all, the association already was hard-pressed to find the womanpower—women still being in the majority—to service three large programs: the piano contest, the massed concert, and the theory exams. Should more be added?

⚜

piano
theory
examination
syllabus

10

A New Way of Life—
The Syllabus Arrives

During the late 1960s and 70s, the nation faced the tragedy of the Vietnam War and the readjustments following the youth rebellion, but despite these, the country was not engulfed with day-to-day interruptions of its basic life as it had been in the world wars and the great depression. The various MTAs throughout the nation were not faced with possible extinction as they had been in the not so distant past.

The age of regional theater, opera, and orchestras was dawning. Public radio and television offered a broad spectrum of music, literature and art. Commercial and private recording thrived. It became possible to hear not only recordings of the standard repertory but large quantities of early and contemporary music. Computers began to enter the scene. The information age was at hand. There was room for new creative fervor.

"A new way of life"[1] for MMTA opened between 1968 and 1970 with the development of a piano syllabus. This single step had far-reaching consequences: marvelous new opportunities for students and a more professional organization for teachers.

The president who led the initial charge, Paul Freed,[2] had long served as judge of MMTA contests. From that experience and from his own teaching he had developed strong ideas about what students needed to know. There were basics which everyone should master. In judging MMTA students, he had observed the presence—or lack—of such fundamentals. Now that a plan for member certification was in place in 1967, the time seemed right for shifting attention from the teachers to the "product" of those teachers: the student.

At the 1968 convention, Freed and his board put forth a plan for the future of MMTA.

1) Increase membership
2) Develop a syllabus
3) Close the profession to unqualified teachers

Paul Freed

The initiative was announced with great fanfare. Members responded with an intensity equal to that long-ago moment when certification was first proposed in 1912. The new proposal carried a price tag of $1,000 for startup. Within a short time, $250 was pledged to the MMTA Development Fund and the association embarked on their new way.

As a first step, Sister Laurian Schumacher compiled a list of Minnesota music teachers. Unaffiliated people on that list were invited to be guests at the 1969 convention. A large attendance ensued and, year by year, membership increased. In 1969, 438 teachers were members. Within five years, as the syllabus program proved its worth, membership reached 600. By 1980, the roster was 701 teachers and by 1989, 849, nearly double the membership two decades earlier.

Publicity and membership, important as they were, had to be backed by a solid core program. Freed, professor of piano at the University of Minnesota, took a three-month leave from his position to work on the project. He examined the two syllabus systems of Canada: the Toronto plan whose publications and examinations covered the whole country and the smaller Western Board plan centered in Manitoba. Using these as models, he wrote a piano syllabus suitable for American use; a syllabus covering eleven stages of development. Level One began with the basic five-note (pentachord) pattern and simple rhythms, together with technical studies and appropriate pieces.

The requirements are as follows:

To be played from memory, ascending and descending, at a moderate tempo with firm, even touch.

a) THE FIVE-NOTE (PENTACHORD) PATTERN: Play in all major and minor keys, legato, hands together. Finish each pattern with the tonic triad.

b) THE FIVE-NOTE (PENTACHORD) PATTERN: Play in all major and minor keys, each hand alone, in two-note slurs as follows:

Then it gradually progressed through the intermediate levels to Level Eleven requiring complex scales, chords, arpeggios and octaves coupled with demanding repertory. Each stage was coordinated with the existing theory program.

Syllabus and studies, scales and arpeggios bring to mind the mechanical aspects of piano playing. The Minnesota project, however, did have broader aims. Even in the First Level the student was asked to play the simple pentachord with staccato and legato, those elements which lead to connection and separation of units of musical thought. Likewise required studies were to show a difference of musical styles. In grading, sheer accuracy had an important place—25 points out of 100—but musicianship (style, phrasing, rhythm, tone quality, pedaling, and ability to explain the music) was given precedence with some 40 points out of 100. When this was coupled with the theory requirements and essays on composers and and historical periods, a comprehension of music not solely as mechanics but as an art emerged.

Students and teachers tested the new syllabus to determine its practicality. Margaret Poole of Toronto explained the Canadian experience.[3] Representatives of Minnesota's colleges and universities reviewed the plans and made suggestions that would ensure basic standards for their entering college students.[4] In short, the new program was subjected to wide-ranging discussion and consideration before its publication.

President Shirley Rediger[5] and her board prepared and submitted grant proposals to cover the costs of the new endeavor. The Bremer Foundation approved a grant of $2,500 to cover costs of publication and the Bush Foundation approved a grant of $12,350 for research and preparation. These generous grants—the largest ever made to a state MTA—allowed MMTA to place a free copy in the hands of all members when the completed work became available in the fall of 1970. From the perspective of several decades later, one can only marvel at the boldness, thorough preparation and energy of its founders.

Shirley Rediger

Ethel Hascall

Rediger called a special meeting in 1970 to establish a unit to deal with the administative and financial issues of the syllabus program: the Minnesota Music Teachers Educational and Charitable Fund. It was "to receive charitable contributions and distribute prizes and funds in ways that would enhance music education." It also handled the administration of the Bush Foundation grant and oversaw the Piano, Theory, and Composition elements of the new plan. The first group of chairmen is listed below.

> Dorothy Harris, Original Composition Contest Chairman
> June Arnold, Theory Examination Chairman
> Justine O'Connor, Theory Committee Chairman
> Ethel Hascall, Chairman of the Piano Syllabus Exams
> Paul Freed, Chairman of Piano Examiners

They were to be followed by other supervisors, groups of volunteers manning these responsible posts, through the next decades.

While in 1970 the theory exams were already functioning, the piano syllabus exams had to be organized from scratch. Hascall[6] traveled to Winnipeg to consult with the leaders of the University of Manitoba in order to understand how the Canadian Western Board administered their program. She found examination, grading and reporting procedures were assumed by the university staff.[7]

Such supervision by college faculties might have been possible in Minnesota but was not approved by MMTA which wanted to keep its long tradition of autonomy. Consequently Hascall had to develop her own report forms and methods. Fortunately colleges and universities of the state offered their facilities and often judges as well. Soon the new way was both functioning and growing.

Year	Registration	Participating Teachers
Spring 1971	387	
1971–1972	691	42
1972–1973	684	50
1973–1974	666	92
§		
1978–1979	1120	169
§		
1988–1989	1509	211

With the new program came a flood of creativity. Newsletters began to feature "Thoughts for Theory." Guna Skujina published four books of *Latvian Melodies for Piano* suitable for sight reading, harmonization and transposition. Justine O'Connor, the spark behind the theory program, put forth four books of *Folksongs for Musicianship*. Mary Davida assembled a six volume series published by Belwin Mills: *Adventures in Time and Space*, designed both as studies and examples of the modern style.[8] The syllabus had arrived. The association was transformed.

MMTA's numerous and growing programs had now reached a point where the association's administrative structures had to change. Work had become as complicated as that of a corporation with demanding schedules and financial responsibilities—all with volunteer help and a few modest honoraria!

In 1973, President Louise Guhl explained the situation.

> One year ago, MMTA adopted two new constitutions, embodying some radical changes in our government. The great need was for more officers and committee people to carry a work load which had become too heavy for the previous form of government. This year over 6000 student registrations were processed for MMTA Auditions, the annual Contest, the Theory Test, and the Syllabus Examinations, each event involving scheduling of time and place, engaging judges and examiners, collecting and disbursing fees, administering the events, and transmitting the results to the teachers.[9]

Again volunteers saved the day. "Our new government has drawn more members into positions of leadership, and their willingness to assume responsibility is a healthy sign."[10]

Louise Guhl

The state began to be recognized around the nation. The Illinois Music Teachers Association made arrangements to buy 500 copies of the syllabus. In 1973, James Bastien in his compendium *How to Teach Piano Successfully* used MMTA as a principal example "because of its highly structured examinations in theory and piano performance"[11] and he highlighted MMTA's system of judging students and its certification standards.[12] Guhl could report after the 1972 national convention:

> "Minnesota is in the very front with its program of student education. While we are carrying out a broad education program, most states are concerned with such problems as collecting dues, getting more student participation, arranging convention programs, etc."[13]

It had been customary to recognize a few outstanding students, so-called "young artists," by presenting them during the Honors Student Concert each year. The number of worthy students in this category rose to the point where, beginning in the the mid-60s, a separate appearance, known as the Young Artist Recital, had to be established. It became a feature of the annual conventions. The program below shows what one could expect. It recognized some 17 pianists, organists and singers as state winners (the teacher's names appear in parentheses). Two competed on the divisional level, Michael

Christopherson at the high school level and Noel Engebretson at the college level. Engebretson won at the West Central Division Competition and received honorable mention in the national competition.

```
                    YOUNG ARTIST RECITAL
                       June 11, 1973
                   College of Saint Catherine

    PRELUDE and TRUMPETING              Roberts
            Deborah Doidge (Avis Marsh)
    ITALIAN CONCERTO (1st Mov't)        Bach
            Kathy Rodel (Sister Patricia Kadlecek)
    SONATA IN D MAJOR (K. 576, 3rd Mov't)   Mozart
            Susan Ferron (Milous Ferlik)
    BALLADE NO. 3 in A-FLAT             Chopin
            Mary Susan Ludwig (Diana Lee Metzker)
    NOW SLEEPS THE CRIMSON PETAL        Quilter
            Sheree Soine, Mezzo Soprano (Alma Stepperud)
                 Deborah Kvittem, Accompanist
    SONATA IN C-MINOR FOR ORGAN         Mendelssohn
            Marilyn Stassen (Gertrude Huffman)
    FISCHERWEISE                        Schubert
            Robin Henry, Contralto (Marguerite Hedges)
                 Jerome Brakke, Accompanist
    DANSE                               Debussy
            Mary Defiel (Sister Mary Ann Hanley)
    UNE BARQUE SUR L'OCÉAN (Miroirs)    Ravel
            Karen Broburg (Gordon Howell)
    L'ISLE JOYEUSE                      Debussy
            Vernon Mooney (Joanne Tierney)
    ME VOICI DANS SON BOUDOIR (Mignon)  Thomas
            Holly Olson, Mezzo Soprano (Marguerite Hedges)
                 Jerome Brakke, Accompanist
    TOCCATA (Suite Gothique)            Boëllmann
            Christine Mattison (Carol Mattison)
    LUSINGHE PIU CARE                   Handel
            Catherine Niosi, Soprano (Marguerite Hedges)
    PRÉLUDE (Pour le Piano)             Debussy
            Anne Leroux (Sister Mary Ann Hanley)
    ALBORADA DEL GRACIOSO (Miroirs)     Ravel
            Michael Christopherson (Harriet Reistad)
            Winner for Minnesota, MTNA High School Audition
    SCARBO (Gaspard de la Nuit)         Ravel
            Noel Engebretson (Paul Freed)
            Winner for Minnesota, MTNA College Audition
            Honorable Mention, National Audition
    TOCCATA (Organ Symphony #5)         Widor
            Phyllis Tellinghuisen (Eileen Bass)
```

Teachers and students were intrigued by the possibilities of creative work recognized in the "new way of life." The composition program began rather modestly but soon was attracting some 80 or more entrants per year. A group of young musicians performing their own winning compositions soon had to be added to the Young Artist Recital.[14] In the concert above, the composition winners appeared in the middle of the program.

FIRST PLACE WINNERS IN ORIGINAL COMPOSITION

Elementary:	WANDERING by Ann Allison (Romaine Conn)
Junior:	VOYAGE by Eric Pazandak (Barbara Smith)
Senior:	TETON SUMMER by James Erickson (Romaine Conn)

FIRST PLACE WINNER IN ORIGINAL COMPOSITION IN WEST CENTRAL DIVISION OF MTNA

Junior:	WILD RIVER by Kathy Semple (Eleanor Yackel)

In the years to follow the early program above, the number of Minnesota students qualifed for competition on divisional and national levels increased dramatically. By 1986, the initial name of Young Artist Recital had to be changed to Honors Recital, an inclusive term for students from junior high school through college levels. The composition students represented on these recitals, however, could start at the elementary school level.

With national acclaim and a published syllabus, the time seemed ripe for MMTA to make another attempt at state recognition. Misunderstandings, however, still existed. The massed piano concerts at Northrop Auditorium gave the public the impression that MMTA was *only* a piano teachers group. Some people looked at the great number of women members and thought of them as housewives who taught a little piano. Many, including the officials of the State Department of Education thought that piano teaching was "just a pin-money source for supplementing family income."[15]

Of course, piano teachers did dominate the association, a perfectly natural occurence. Many if not most parents concerned with serious musical education insisted that a child have a piano background before or during study of another instrument. It had enormous advantages. As early as 1911, the distinguished musician, Donald Ferguson, spoke of the piano as:

> the instrument which, better than any other, is able to treat a mu-
> sical composition in its entirety as an art-work. The piano is,
> without doubt, by far the greatest medium for the dissemination
> of culture, and an understanding of its enormous literature would
> be in itself, a sufficient foundation for the immediate apprecia-
> tion of all other purely musical forms.[16]

The piano had practical advantages. It used two standard clefs, bass and treble. The pianist did not have to struggle to read an unfamiliar clef. as a clari-
netist, violinist or any musician used to reading a single line of notes might.
The pianist already had command of larger patterns of music. It is this command of the complete fabric of music which is essential in advanced study.

In truth, most college music theory courses required keyboard harmony as
a way of hearing and understanding complex harmonies and intricate
polyphony. The piano keyboard served to bring musical sound and physical
action into the complexities of music theory thus removing it from the realm
of abstraction. As Madeleine Titus said: "Awareness of visual shapes in notation and on the keyboard, of tactile shapes in the hand, and of aural shapes
inside the head should be an outcome of the integration of theory into piano
study."[17]

Now that the goals of MMTA had been codified, defined, and brought to
action, the association once more appealed to state education officials for
recognition.

> 1970 *Convention Address* by Dr. David Price, Music Consultant to the
> Minnesota State Board of Education.
> *Panel Discussion by this Music Consultant, the Chairman
> of the University of Minnesota Music Department, a
> Superintendent of Schools and a State Legislator.*
> "Is the musically talented child in Minnesota given the
> opportunity for pre-college development to which he
> is entitled?"
>
> 1971 *National Survey* of State Commissioners of *Education.*
> 1972 *Meetings* with the Professions Development Unit of the State
> Board of Education.
> 1973 *Task Force* on certification of public school music teachers
> includes MMTA President, Louise Guhl.

Guhl spoke powerfully to the state education authorities from her position
as head of piano pedagogy at the University of Minnesota. She got only partial results, only a small step forward. Local school officials would be free to

establish programs within their boundaries but on request, not as state policy. This solution agreed with legal restrictions and represented the only possible avenue that MMTA had and still has available today. It may indeed be
the only equitable response: a step by the state which requires an answering
step by the music teachers themselves.

Except for the city of Edina, very few local groups took any action on this
decision. Some years before this verdict, the private teachers, superintendant
of schools and director for educational development of that city developed
the Edina Applied Music Program.

(1) Any Edina Public School student may take this program for
full credit. The fee for lessons will be the responsibility of the
parents.

(2) Secondary students may register for one or more semesters in
this program and may receive regular course credit. This credit
may serve in lieu of the State music requirement. Two semester credits may apply toward graduation.

(3) Elementary school children may participate in this program
in lieu of the music activity with the approval of the appropriate teacher and principal of the school.

(4) Edina Schools application and report forms will be used.

(5) Any instrumental teacher who has been certified by the
Minnesota Music Teachers Association and holds a certificate in Category One (Doctor's or Master's degree in Music
with five years' teaching experience) or Category Two (Bachelor's degree in Music with five years teaching experience) may
participate in this program. Other music teachers must hold
a degree in their field from an accredited college and must
have private teaching experience. Current members of major
professional orchestras or professors of Minnesota colleges
may also participate.[18]

The long struggle of MMTA for official credit within the schools thus ended
with these guidelines, the carefully reasoned view of school administrators, a
plan available to any local group seeking official recognition. Edina, one of
the most prominent school districts of the state pointed the way out of the impasse that MMTA had faced for many decades.

By 1973, Minnesota had made a successful transition to its new way of
life. There remained, however, certain practical steps. President Mary Davida
Wood[19] and committees began to develop syllabi for voice and orchestral instruments. She and Sondra Howe developed a non-keyboard theory syllabus

Mary Davida Wood, CSJ

Marguerite Hoffman

for those students not studying piano. She and Jean Hegland, theory chairman, took the new systems out to six of the eight districts of the state in a successful education program.

Each year brought another hundred or so students and about thirty new teachers into the syllabus program. Not only had the syllabus arrived but it had succeeded to the point where the association was forced to find new ways of governance. To cope with its success, MMTA decided to spread the all-too-numerous tasks among more members. It also decided to break with the tradition of having college faculty in the presidential position and instead began alternating college teachers and independent teachers in that post.[20] There was now a chance for all to progress to the highest office. The practical result was that gradually women presidents began to predominate, the reverse of earlier days.

Work had so expanded that it would have been very expensive to continue MMTA's business affairs with State Organization Services. The next president, Marguerite Hoffman,[21] as head of a music school in Rochester, Minnesota, was accustomed to administration. She persuaded the board and members that the time had come for MMTA to invest in office equipment and establish its own General Secretary and Office. While at first, this required borrowing money, it has proven itself over and over again. Today the Central Office is firmly organized with enough room to stock the large supply of association materials. It can respond quickly to teachers' calls for syllabi and workbooks.

As the first eight years passed, teachers found that there were certain re-curring problems within the syllabus—especially for the very young. Many, if not most, of the young aspirants found that they could not master the five-finger positions (the pentachords) in all twenty-four major and minor keys during the first year of study. This was easily remedied in a revision that al-lowed this requirement to be spread over several levels.

Another more difficult problem arose when students were not able to cor-rectly read at sight examples of the syllabus test. Consequently a group of teachers—and later a committee of MMTA—began serious study of how to present the extremely complicated notation of music in a series of graduated steps. The research and investigation extended over more than a half a decade and will be further chronicled in the following chapter.

One of the most important steps came in teaching reading by musical in-tervals, a practice being adopted nationally as well as in Minnesota. Students could see quickly that seconds—steps—went from line to space or space to line, thirds went from line to line or space to space.

In this excerpt, the melody notes go by steps until the second measure when they proceed "down a third."

In this excerpt the larger leap from line to line skipping a line is "down a fifth," then by steps until in the second measure which is, of course, "down a third." Students could acquaint themselves one by one with the sound of these intervals, with their feel at the keyboard, and gradually with the letter names, a three-fold experience which reinforced learning.[22]

President Gordon Howell[23] of Bethel College, had been trained under the Canadian system and was experienced in judging. He, along with many vol-unteers, supervised the small but significant changes of the syllabus in the re-vision of 1978 and began to use test examples incorporating ideas from the teachers who were researching music reading.

Gordon Howell

The short space of a decade had brought a new way of life—a way stem-ming from the syllabus. MMTA had found a pathway toward higher stan-dards of musicianship, a means for creative teaching, and an affirmation of basic musical values. A boon to teachers and students alike.

✦

MMTA 80th Anniversary. The Grand Piano Birthday Cake. Henry Steinway and Phyllis Peabody, MMTA President, 1979–1981.

11

A Work in Progress

In the last two decades of the twentieth century, a number of moderate-sized towns experienced a growth of commerce that made them into regional centers offering possibilities formerly known only in the largest centers. Some even became convention centers. The Metropolitan Area expanded into the third tier of suburbs—Burnsville, Apple Valley, Eden Prairie, Plymouth, Maple Grove, Blaine, Shoreview, Cottage Grove, Inver Grove Heights, Eagan—areas still allied to the Twin Cities but with links to their own and surrounding communities.[1]

Along with economic expansion came an educational and cultural one. The five state colleges which had started early in the history of the state as normal schools now gained the rank of universities. A system of eighteen community colleges as well as thirty-four technical colleges was completed. The Minnesota Legislature supported regional art councils.

Private colleges recognized the performance arts. Macalester College inaugurated the Janet Wallace Center in 1965. St. Catherine's in St. Paul led the way in large auditoriums with O'Shaughnessy Auditorium in 1970. Later St. Scholastica in Duluth built the Mitchell Auditorium and St. Benedict's at St. Joseph built the Benedicta Center. At the end of the century, few colleges, private or public, were without an art and music center.

A system of public radio and television stations brought outstanding cultural events into home and community. Minnesota soon became a household word around the nation as Garrison Keillor offered a variety of homespun stories, music, and humor. Even New Englanders on Cape Cod gathered around the radio on Saturday nights with the gang from Lake Woebegon.

The theater movement grew until the Twin Cities became a Mecca for actors. It offered "more theater seats per capita than any other city in the world."[2] Even in smaller places theater developed: the Cherry Creek Theater in southern Minnesota, the L'Homme Dieu in the north.[3]

Distinguished small presses—Milkweed, Graywolf, New Rivers, Nodin and others—began publishing. A number of these were drawn to the state by grants offered to non-profit groups by Minnesota foundations. Individuals active in writing formed local units and published small literary magazines. Courses, prizes, workshops and readings helped fuel the movement. *Minnesota Literature* became the newsletter and calendar for an impressive group of writers. One could now buy Minnesota poetry, novels and stories at bookshops around the state.

The Minnesota Historical Society remade itself in these years. It sponsored many local historical sites and encouraged preservation of traditions, many stemming from various ethnic groups of Minnesota. Recordings of voyageur songs, polka, Norwegian-American music, and Ojibway music, encouraged people to experience the musical heritage of the state. With the inauguration of the new History Center in 1992, the society offered unparalleled research opportunities into the past—including the early archives of MMTA—and into the present as well in interactive exhibits and live performances. Soon the society was recognized as prime in the nation and its director, Nina Archabal was awarded the National Medal of Arts and Humanities by the President of the United States.

"Outstate Minnesota" had now been transformed into "Greater Minnesota." Gone was the second-rate status suggested by "outstate" and in its place was "greater"—not just a bit of idle boosterism but a statement of the truth. This cultural revolution, now so apparent, had come about so gradually that only in retrospect do we recognize it.

As we might expect, MMTA transformed itself during these energetic years. In fact, the association embarked on so many programs that the historian is hard pressed to convey them to the reader. MMTA had been like a great tree with a few branches; it now had become more like a venerable, mature tree with firm side boughs leading to still more branches.

Let us begin with the accomplishments in the "outreach" program, so long a function of the association. A few leaders in outlying communities began to invite local teachers to meet together to study and learn, and to make opportunities for their students. By 1999 students and teachers could find encouragement and help far from the Twin Cities. The accompanying map shows the present state of MMTA's outreach into Greater Minnesota, a remarkable change from the feeble attempts to organize by counties at the beginning of the century. Here was that "radiating" of musical knowledge and opportunity that Charles Henry Mills had called for in 1912.

A goodly portion of this radiating into local areas came when Marian Hutt and succeeding presidents visited outlying areas and found them thankful that the Twin Cities was coming to them instead of vice versa. The election of leaders who lived "outstate" or in outlying suburbs, Phyllis Peabody of

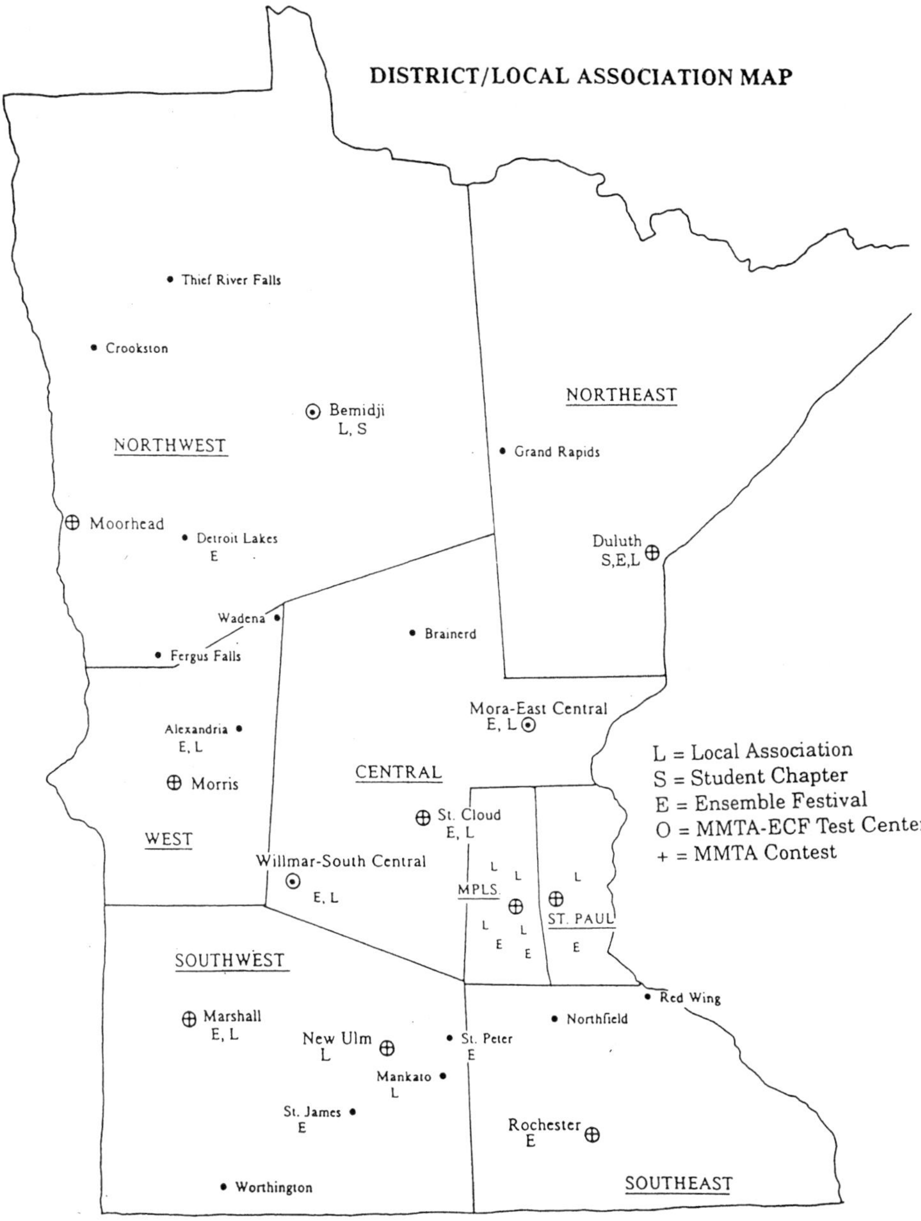

DISTRICT/LOCAL ASSOCIATION MAP

- Thief River Falls

- Crookston

NORTHEAST

⊙ Bemidji
L, S

NORTHWEST

• Grand Rapids

⊕ Moorhead

• Detroit Lakes
E

Duluth
S,E,L ⊕

Wadena •

• Brainerd

• Fergus Falls

Mora-East Central
E, L ⊙

Alexandria •
E, L

CENTRAL

L = Local Association
S = Student Chapter
E = Ensemble Festival
O = MMTA-ECF Test Center
+ = MMTA Contest

⊕ Morris

⊕ St. Cloud
E, L

WEST

Willmar-South Central
⊙
E, L

L
L
L

MPLS.
⊕

⊕
ST. PAUL

L
E

SOUTHWEST

L
E

E

⊕ Marshall
E, L

New Ulm ⊕
L

• St. Peter
E

• Red Wing

• Northfield

Mankato •
L

St. James •
E

Rochester ⊕
E

• Worthington

SOUTHEAST

Long Lake and Ruth Anderson of New Ulm, showed a growing recognition of Greater Minnesota. Then in 1987 newly-instituted "ensemble festivals" proved especially popular throughout the entire state.

These performances of piano duets by students who could enjoy music without the burden of being judged or of having to memorize their pieces became special occasions for pianists. Students would even ask during the summer what compositions they could perform the next year. Young musicians at all levels of advancement shared in the enjoyment. Parents were delighted. Teachers found that through ensembles such essentials as counting the meter of the music improved as did the feeling for rhythm.

The chart below shows how Greater Minnesota has responded.

Locale	Date	Programs	Entries	Teachers
St. Cloud	11/07/98	6	102	14
Pine City-Mora	10/31/98	1	22	6
Duluth	11/15/98	2	30	10
Detroit Lakes	10/24/98	3	35	4
Rochester	11/07/98	4	69	12
Marshall	10/31/98	9	163	12
Willmar	11/08/98	2	20	8
SW St. James	10/31/98	4	95	8
SW St. Peter	11/14/98	2	44	9
Alexandria	11/14/98	3	42	7
TC Minneapolis	11/07/98	5	88	14
TC St. Paul	11/21/98	4	65	14
TC Shakopee	11/21/98	3	45	11
Olivia	11/15/98	4	45	5

The St. Cloud program, which will be used here as an example, is one of the most active.[4] A recent program presented over one hundred students, pupils of eighteen teachers, who performed in the Recital Hall of St. Cloud State University. One of the performances, the 11:00 AM recital of older students will give a taste of what was performed: some accepted standards of the concert repertory and some pieces that as one title had it were "Just Plain Fun."

As more statewide programs were initiated and more and more local activities became established, the MMTA board changed its focus from oversight of details—what President Russell Harris called "counting paper clips" or "deciding which copying machine screw to procure"[5]—to a function of

Stars and Stripes Forever	Sousa
Lauren Copeland, Jacob Benda	
Rag Weed Rag	Averre
Casey Angell, Stephanie Bales	
Waltz	Diabelli
Ryan Antony, Casie Antony	
Sand Dunes	Mier
Leah Ewing, Ann Chow	
Wistful Waltz	Anderson
Laura Foster, Shelly Stemper	
Mazurka	Becucci
Casey Angell, Ezzie Angell	
Spanish Tornado	Noona
Lulu Hu, Samantha Pallaunsch	
All-American Hometown Band	Noona
Dan Cyson, Joe Engebritson	
Down Home Dance	Noona
Maggie Lalor, Ben Copeland	
In the Hall of the Mountain King	Grieg, arr. Clark
Alex Warzecha, Stuart McCarter	
Changing Places	Burnam
Nicholas Gangi, Micah Bot-Miller	
Sand Dunes	Mier
Kari Pfannenstein, Courtney Kunstad	
Remember When	Wandall
Nicole Hansen, Brynn Foster	
Hoedown	Copland
Ryan Antony, Jed Angell	

St. Cloud Ensemble Festival Program

policy maker and administrator. In early years, it had been possible to list five or six principal officers on the letterhead and seven or eight district chairmen along the side of a single page of official stationery. By the 1990s MMTA had a Board of Directors and the MMTA Educational and Charitable Foundation a Board of Trustees, each with ten officers apiece. Additional work was shouldered by "designated officers and committees" which as of 1999 comprised:

Advertising Chair
Articles of Incorporation and Bylaws
Audiovisual Library
Calendar Editor

Centennial Heritage Committee
College Liason
Historian
International Study Tour
Liason - High School Accompanist Certificates
Long Range Planning Chair
Music Technology Chair
Newsletter Editor
Nominating Committee
Publicity Chair
Resource File Administrator
Volunteer Resource Chair/Volunteer Recognition Chair
Affiliate Members Chair
Certification Chair
New Members, Student Members
New Member Mentor Chair
Membership Renewal Chair
Student Chapter Chair (with several chapter chairs)
Community Outreach
Independent Music Teachers Forum Chair
Local Associations Chair
MTNA Foundation Chair
MTNA Student Composition Chair
Coordinator of State MTNA Auditions/Collegiate Auditions Chair
MTNA High School Auditions Chair
MTNA Junior High Auditions Chair

Even this impressive list does not include the committee members who worked under the various "chairs," or the workers associated with sixteen local associations scattered over the state. What is even more awesome is that the organization ran with volunteers. As president Kathleen Hasse said in 1999, "I know of no other organization that accomplishes so much and does it so well, with volunteers only, and without paid professional staff."[6]

Concurrent with Minnesota's leap forward, the national association made bold new moves completing the chain between country-wide sources and small locales. MTNA had served from 1876 on as a shelter for a great variety of musicians and music teachers. Gradually as musical culture spread throughout the country, more specialized groups were organized such as the American Musicological Society, the College Music Society, the National Association of Teachers of Singing, the Music Library Association, and many, many more.

A committee takes a break as they plan the 1988 convention
(from l. to r.) Sharon Kaplan, Joan Pickard, Raeanna Gislason,
Sandra Saliny, Bettye Ware, Tom Allen, Cora Barr

These groups with unique interests gradually set up their own units—apart from MTNA—much as the Music Educators had done in the 1930s.[7]

More and more, as specialized organizations found other homes, the national association became the voice of the studio teacher in college and community. With this change in clientele, MTNA began to establish rewards for students, certification for teachers and standards for both groups—the same programs that MMTA was creating. State and National now acted in tandem.[8]

Many of the initiatives on the national level began as MTNA made preparations for its centennial year of 1976. Several music firms offered awards. In the case of the Baldwin Piano Company, the prize was for junior piano achievement. Gradually recognition was extended to high school and collegiate levels. In specific organizational projects MTNA began the following:

1965   High School Auditions (including theory and reading fluency)
1967   National Teacher Certification Plan
1972   Student Composition Award
1972   MTNA Foundation

A new outlook began with a new name. The old, rather imprecise, term of "private" or "studio" teacher was dropped. Community teachers became known as independent music teachers, business people as well as devoted musicians. In 1972, MTNA established a forum for these teachers and the following year Minnesota appointed Carol Mattison as first chair of its own Independent Music Teachers Forum. These newly-recognized people had previously had only individual, often lonely, voices. Now the associations, state and national, began to consider insurance, taxes, retirement and the many items that would make the teacher secure and truly professional.

MMTA focused upon things that would help this part of their membership in their teaching. A whole series of books for students appeared under the auspices of the MMTA Educational and Charitable Foundation.

> *Sightplaying,* 6 levels & a book of sample tests
> *Music Theory Workbook* for students, 6 levels
> *Music Theory Workbook* for teachers, 6 levels
> Sample tests and recorded examples
> A series of syllabi, those for Flute, Voice, Organ, Guitar, etc.

Each of these grew out of years of preparation and devoted work by committees which prepared materials, subjected them to trial, revised them, and finally published them in a professional format made possible by computer printing. Each level took at least a year in initial preparation and then several more years before a definitive version was reached.

The sightplaying books, for example, grew out of the realization that few skills could be more important than sightplaying to the student. A skilled sight reader was a musically literate person who could learn independently and could accompany other musicians.

The piano syllabus from the very first had a sight-reading component.

> Play a simple tune in five-finger position, using half and quarter notes. The first phrase will be for the right hand in the treble clef and the second for the left hand in the bass clef. (1970 *Syllabus,* Level 1)

> Play a simple tune in pentachord position using half and quarter notes. First phrase will be for the right hand in the treble clef and the second part for the left hand in the bass clef. The example will be in F Major, D Major, E-Flat Major or E Minor. (1978 *Syllabus,* Level 1)

In practice, teachers found that even in the resulting simple music, young students were confronted with too many choices.

It was necessary to determine exactly how these students learned the complex notation of music. Many six-year-old to nine-year-old beginning pianists had no knowledge of fractions and even had difficulty orienting themselves

Jean Hegland
MMTA president, 1981–1983

Marian M. Hutt
MMTA president, 1985–1987

Ruth V. Anderson
MMTA president, 1987–1989

to the treble and bass clefs. The first steps toward establishing rudiments for both sight reading and accompanying were taken by a committee independent of MMTA. This group not only worked on methods and on testing but also solicited funds.[9]

The committee members could see that the program needed to grow and that they had neither the resources nor the strength to take it where it needed to go. It needed the prestige of an established group. MMTA seemed the proper place for this essential program. In the season of 1976 a Sight Reading and Accompanying Committee under the supervision of the Educational and Charitable Foundation of MMTA was instituted. This official group worked diligently for years, 1976–1985, formulating standards and testing students. The members found that young students needed secure guideposts if they were to be successful—and "success" was essential if these youngsters were to gain confidence and real ability.

After 1979, the committee produced a set of five folders, Levels A-E with exact descriptions, daily speed tests, flash cards, and musical examples. The contrast between this "new, early program designed for the student with only one year of piano lessons" and the previous general standards quoted above reveals how remarkable the work of the committee was.

It would be too lengthy to explain here the details of the various levels and how they coordinated with MMTA's performance and theory programs. We can, however, look briefly at an example from the beginning steps of Level A issued in 1979.

> For three pieces of sight reading:
> *Rhythm*
>   a) only quarter and half notes used throughout the piece
>   b) dotted half and whole notes used only at ends of phrases
>   c) no rests
>   d) meters 2/4, 3/4, and 4/4 or a combination
> *Accuracy*
>   a) each hand makes its initial entry from a fixed point
>   middle c, f below middle c, or g above middle c
>   b) no ledger lines except for middle c
>   c) no key signatures
>   d) no accidentals
>   e) no repeated notes in the melody line
>   f) intervals of 2nds and 5ths only

One can see how greatly this differs from the all-too-general description of the original syllabus and how encouraging it would be to the first-year youngster. It gave a priceless sense of security.

Each level of difficulty beyond this beginning stage was carefully planned for natural advancement and for coordination with MMTA's theory program. Eventually the series was revised and presented in six levels. Along the way, the attempt to incorporate accompanying into the testing program had to be abandoned because that art was too complex to be structured into a test. As of 1999, MMTA is giving recognition through certificates for accompanist's work but not trying to codify and test that skill.

The *Music Theory Workbooks* were developed within the structure of MMTA. In 1970, when the piano syllabus was first published, a theory program had already been functioning for five years. There was not, however, a smoothly-spaced increase in difficulty as the student moved from level to level nor even agreement on the difficulty of single levels. Once again, volunteers plunged into revision, expansion, and testing that would make the program more effective.[10]

Teachers originally had reservations, even fears, about aural awareness and ear training exercises not because they doubted their value but they wondered how they could be incorporated into limited lesson time and into the ever more complicated schedules of students. The post-syllabus committees however made the bold decision to fashion theory instruction around three components including this controversial one.

> 1) Written material
> 2) Aural Awareness/Ear Training
> 3) Keyboard material

Members who developed the program started with those musical ideas which the young student would find in their repertoire pieces and in their sightplaying. They expected the youngest student to be able to write pentachords—the first five notes of each scale—which were the basic material of their performing pieces.[11] The student was playing and hearing these patterns; notation came naturally and "aural awareness" followed likewise. Coupled with this ability to handle musical pitches came rhythmic practice on short patterns—once again following a restricted number of patterns. MMTA had achieved real "adventures in time and space."[12]

What a huge difference between this "new, early program" and instruction at the beginning of the century. Then the young student was given a set of abstract rules—letter names, key signatures, fractional values of notes—which she or he was expected to apply. Now the young student began with certain anchor points and built by playing music and hearing its structure. Music theory had become as "practical" as Paul Oberg had desired, as much of a "tool" as Guy Duckworth had demonstrated. The hopes of the 1950s had become the achievement of the 1980s.

Mary Ann Hanley, CSJ
MMTA president, 1989–1991

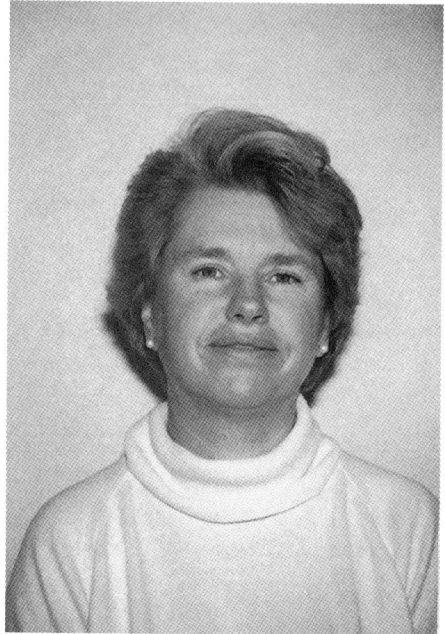

Kay G. Koehnen
MMTA president, 1991–1993

Raeanna Gislason
MMTA president, 1993–1995

The theory program turned out to be a great success as teachers found that the theory, performance and sightplaying activities supported one another and led to more secure learning. The report for years 1996–1999 shows the acceptance of MMTA's plan.[13]

KEYBOARD THEORY EXAMS
Annual Report: 1998–1999 Carolyn W. Zarling, NCTM

Total Students Registered			
1995–1996	1996–1997	1997–1998	1998–1999
1,686	1,675	1,705	1,612
Total Test Centers			
21	21	23	25
Total students registered, by level			
Level I	1,033	1,051	990
Level II	430	434	429
Level III	154	166	155
Level IV	54	50	28
Level V	4	5	7
Level VI	0	1	3
Total students registered, by district			
SW New Ulm	105	110	87
SW Marshall	86	81	82
SE Rochester	154	138	145
EC Mora	44	22	23
C St. Cloud	152	159	142
C Wilmar	30	33	21
W Morris	57	51	42
NE Duluth	47	64	39
NW Moorhead	73	82	67
NW Bemidji	22	44	34
TC Bethel	905	921	851
TC St. Paul Park	–	–	6
TC Shakopee	–	–	73

From the earliest days of developing a music theory program, the committee and teachers felt that there might be too much emphasis on conventional harmony. Still it was difficult to work twentieth-century practices into a theory syllabus. The students were, however, hearing modern music and they were performing it in repertory selections. As a further possibility, a growing number of MMTA teachers began to train their students in composition, a fascinating topic and one that allowed students freedom to incorporate some features beyond conventional practice.

The youngest composition students frequently began with little descriptive pieces—Pagoda, Leprechaun Festival, A Sad and Happy Day, Elephant in the Snow, Frog Jump—usually in some simple "theme-contrast-theme" form. As they grew older and gained acquaintance with more complex forms, they wrote in genres that they were studying in performance: variations, sonatinas, dances and such. They learned to write musical scores correctly and have benefited from the judges' comments which cover all of the technical and imaginative aspects of their submissions. A number of MMTA students have been winners in divisional competition but none has yet won first place in the national auditions for compositions.

We have now briefly described for you, the reader, the great branches for one portion of our MMTA tree, the boughs relating to student opportunities. The time has now come to examine another portion, those branches pertaining to the expansion of the association and the profession.

Certification was particularly essential for the independent teacher. College and institutional teachers go through a screening process and are continually evaluated by their peers. The individual teacher could rely only on a somewhat vague public recognition or a system devised by MMTA or MTNA.

Since 1913, Minnesota had been a leader in certifying its members. In the 1950s, the system of three levels—Graduate Accredited, Accredited, and Associate—was set up under Chiuminatto. In 1972, this system was strengthened by requiring each of the accredited members to renew their certification every five years with proof of in-service education, public performances by teacher or student, leadership, and professional involvement. In 1980, the system was further strengthened by the elimination of the so-called equivalency clause, that the certification committee might judge certain qualities and background to be equivalent to a degree.[14]

During the last decades of the century, the national organization established its own system of certification. Numerous problems arose as Minnesota tried to mesh with the national program. Gradually an accord was reached. Teachers could qualify for the NCTM, National Certified Teacher of Music. Minnesota enrollment in this program grew slowly. Learning and applying the Minnesota syllabus left little time for MTNA certification. In 1975, 67 Minnesota members were nationally certified but by 1999, 174 held the NCTM ranking, about one-fifth of the total membership.

President Mary Ann Hanley studied the history of Minnesota certification and proposed a system that would allow for national standards, demanding state standards, and would still welcome those teachers who were at the be-

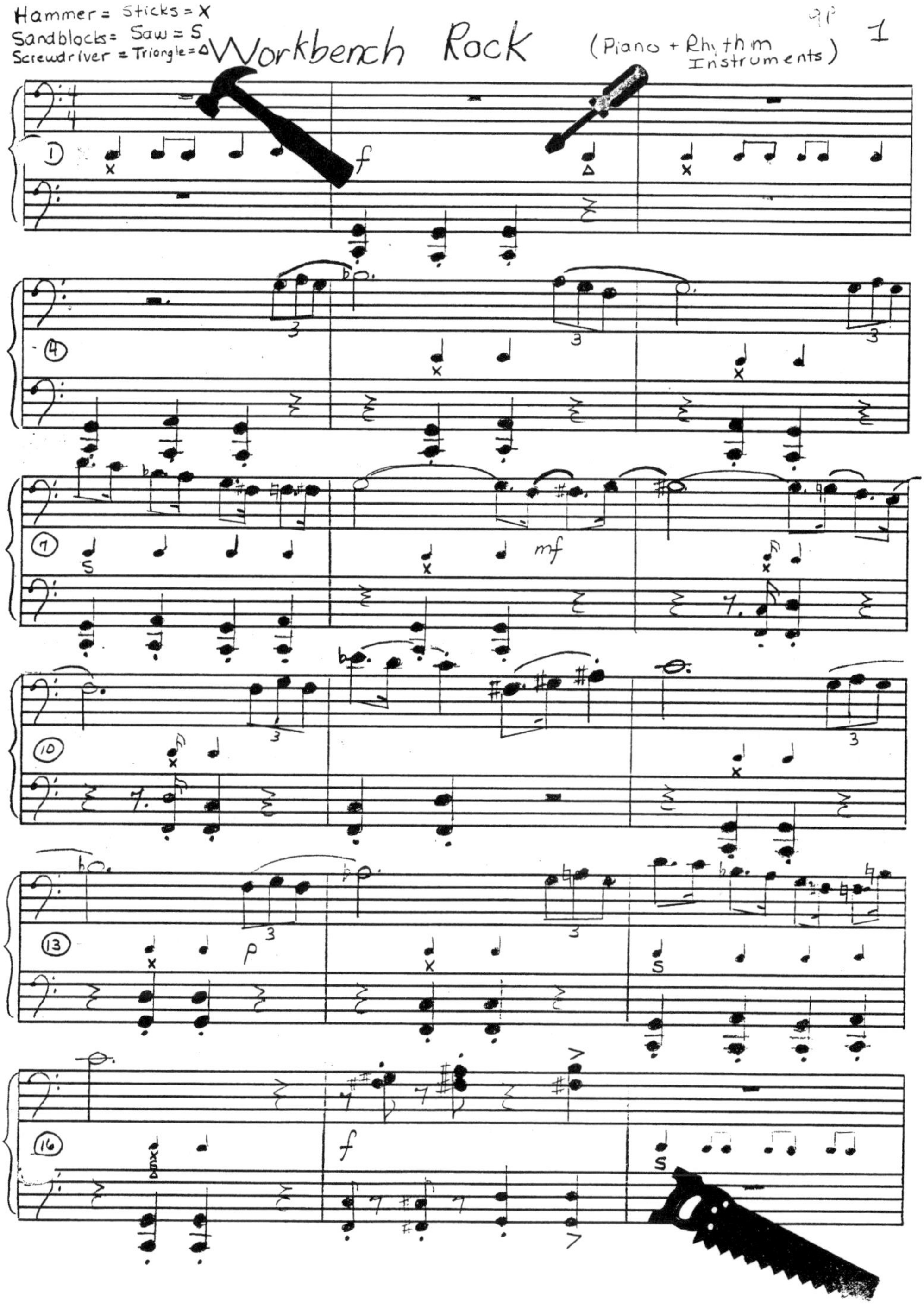

Winning Primary Division Composition by Jeffrey Bina

ginning of their careers and who were still learning. This resulted in the current system with three classes of certified teachers and three classes of members.

Master Certificate:	Master's Degree, 5 years of private study for college credit.
Professional Certificate:	Bachelor's Degree, 3 years of private study for college credit.
Associate Certificate:	3 years of private study for college credit, theory, history & pedagogy
Associate Membership:	8 years of private study (3 years after high school), theory
Provisional Membership	
Student Membership	

In 1999, out of a total membership of 848 teachers, two-thirds were certified teachers; the remainder were members on their way to certification.

To adequately serve this varied population, MMTA began to hold multi-session conventions with two or three events going on at the same time. Teachers at various levels could choose the most useful topic. This was first suggested in 1984 by Russell Harris and succeeding presidents gradually developed that format. Ruth Anderson revised the convention brochure from a small program to a large, 8 ½-x-11" presentation in a spiral binding. This gave space for biographies of the clinicians, pages of notes on the sessions, and complete reports of MMTA—in short, an invaluable resource. Mary Ann Hanley carried this a step further by centering the convention around a particular theme, in this first case "A Global Perspective." Themes since have included such things as "A Focus on American Music," "Musical Imagery," and "Bach to Jazz," among others.

The teaching profession, radically changed by information technology, took on a new look in the 1990s. A number of independent music teachers acquired computers. MMTA appointed its first Technology Chair.

Frustration accompanied the first attempts because there were so few computer programs devoted to music. As one teacher said, "I thought I might have to learn to program. . . and one of my sixth-graders offered to teach me."[15] Gradually, however, it became possible for students to hear digitally recorded music and study composers' lives through CD-Roms. They could reinforce their knowledge of music theory through drills and games. Soon they could use a midi keyboard, one that would record in musical notation their own performance and which also allowed them to record and print their own compositions or one part of a duet which they could use when their partner

Mary A. Brandenburg
MMTA president, 1995–1997

Kathleen H. Hasse
MMTA president, 1997–1999

Patricia Nortwen
MMTA president, 1999–2001

Studio in the Johnson School of Music, 1902

was absent. A number of teachers prepared a separate "theory room" where students could work at that topic before or after their lesson at the "live" instrument.

The illustrations show what a leap has been made from a teaching studio of Gustavus Johnson in his school established in 1898 to the studio of Florence Blattner today. Teachers soon found that computer E-mail service was a great way of keeping in touch. One of the present chairs of a committee is able to access her entire group through E-mail. A few of the most enterprising have even prepared programs and web sites that allow them to do all of the scheduling of lessons, bookeeping, calendar of contest dates, in short, all of the chores that attend keeping a studio.

MMTA itself has now established its own web site which allows teachers to join the association, order books, keep track of current events, place themselves on a list of available teachers, and many other services linked to this "home page." MTNA has similar services. At the national convention in Washington, DC, in 1994, the technology sessions were attended by the "greatest number of members to date" and that year *American Music Teacher*, the official organ of MTNA devoted a whole issue to technology

Studio of Florence A. Blattner, 1999

The new information world was enlarging the perspective of teachers and so were European Study Tours, begun by MMTA in 1987. Organized and accompanied by a professional tour leader, each tour had a knowledgeable teacher, usually from one of the colleges. Members spent four sessions with the leader studying the topic during the year preceding the tour. Instruction continued even on the bus when the leader offered information and frequently played tapes of pertinent music. Around thirty people took the tours each of the years offered.

    1987 Central Europe, 26 July–13 August
    1989 Italy, 15 June–2 July
    1991 France, 4–24 July
    1993 England, Wales & Scotland, 7–24 July
    1995 Spain & Portugal, 27 July–15 August
    1997 Scandinavia, 24 June–13 July
    1999 Belgium & Netherlands, 15 July–4 August

A few of the occasions are illustrated here; many more—concerts, visits to instrumental museums, conversations with musicians, art works—rest in the

In Portugal: Learning how violins are made

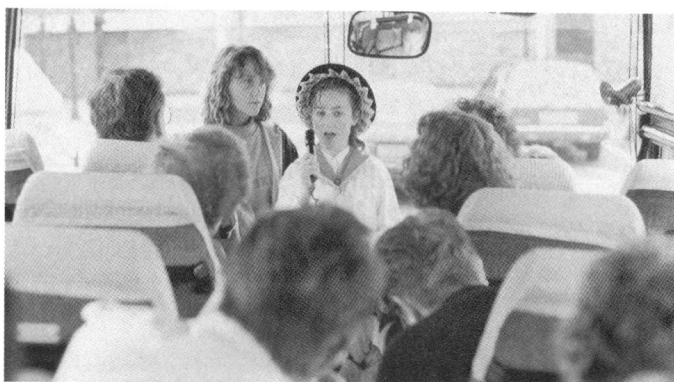

On the bus: Listening to a little Welsh girl singing folksongs

In Edinburgh: Colin Kingsley teaching about harpsichords

minds of the participants. Tour members saw the tarantella danced, learned how violins are made, and captured the spirit of flamenco music. They returned with explanations for their students. A picture of FERMATA as an Italian bus stop and RITARDANDO as a "slow" sign for traffic stuck in their students' minds better than any traditional definition could.

The Independent Music Teacher taking advantage of all of these MMTA programs was not entirely independent. She spent many hours in association work. Members had from the very first been convinced that music was a special art—at first even called "divine." Statements of idealism appeared frequently in the *Newsletters*.

> Music is a moral law. It gives a soul to the universe, wings to the mind, flight to the imagination, a charm to sadness, gaiety and life to everything. It is the essence of order, and leads to all that is good, just, and beautiful, of which it is the invisible but nevertheless dazzling passionate and eternal form.[16]

Statements such as the above from Plato are more than miniature pep-talks; they are principles which have sustained teachers through both difficult and joyous moments; have helped them in demanding organizational work.

MMTA could see the results of its labors recognized beyond the borders of Minnesota. In the 1980s, Minnesota students began to win national auditions. In 1985, the first winner, a remarkably gifted musician, Brian Krinke, won first place in violin performance. He has since gone on to study both violin and piano at Curtis Institute and is now Associate Concertmaster of the Buffalo Symphony Orchestra. In 1995, Jeffrey Graves of Hutchinson, Minnesota, became the national winner for brass instruments. He received his bachelor's degree from Bemidji State University. He earned a master's degree from Ball State University, and is currently finishing his Doctor of Musical Arts at the University of Michigan. He teaches as an adjunct faculty member at Bowling Green.[17]

MMTA has kept not only an outreach program for its members but an ongoing commitment to the wider music community. For over forty years, it has made an annual gift to the Minnesota Orchestra and for lesser periods of time to other outstanding professional groups. In recognition of the association's century-long interest in composition and of Minnesota as the headquarters of the American Composers Forum, MMTA has commissioned piano music from Minnesota composers. In 1982, for instance, Carol Barnett's *Dragons* for piano, 4 hands, was premiered and published by Belwin Mills. She is now working on a trio or quartet—to include piano as one of the instruments—for the Centennial Convention of 2001. In recent years members

Brian Krinke

Jeffrey Graves

Carol Barnett

have composed piano duets to be performed by the twenty pianos of the Honors Student Concert.

Coupled with this outreach to the musical organizations has been a growing presence within MTNA. In the late 1970s, Minnesotans helped to write the national theory syllabus. More recently, Gordon Howell served for two years as chair of the National and Divisional Certification Boards and Raeanna Gislason served a similar term as chair of the National Independent Music Teachers Forum.

At the same time of all of these initiatives for students and teachers, MMTA was building for the future through its Educational and Charitable Foundation. Not only had the foundation handled the development of syllabi, the publication of books, and the awarding of prizes, but it had been amassing funds to be eventually used for the betterment of music and the encouragement of students. Its treasury began with small funds donated by members. Some donated honoraria they would otherwise have received. Devoted, long-time teachers increased the funds by substantial gifts: Gladys Markley donated $5,000 for theory awards; Bertha Ask, at her death at age 100 (1983), willed $5,000 "with love and well wishes." Through the years, members organized various money-raising activities—the sale of T-shirts was one of the biggest successes. Careful management and wise investment brought the funds to a substantial total by 1999. With this capital MMTA is in the midst of planning how to support deserving students.

Each president starting with 1970, however, had to fight with the Internal Revenue Service over the tax-exempt status of the Educational and Charitable Foundation. In 1970 at the time of its inception, MMTA's Educational and Charitable Foundation was mistakenly registered as a "private foundation," totally independent of its creating body. In the last year through the work of Kathy Hasse and her board, the matter has been reviewed and the Educational and Charitable Foundation Association is now properly classified as a "supporting foundation," an action retroactive to 1970. It is now known as the Minnesota Music Teachers Foundation. This change meant that MMTA had to assume some of the supervising and publishing functions previously allotted to the original foundation. Other changes will be necessary as MMTA adjusts to its new responsibilities and as the MMTA Foundation assumes its full role.

The last two decades, a time of diversity and growth, have seen the association stretching out in many directions. Today's luxuriant tree with its many branches would astonish founders Willard Patton, Clarance Marshall, Gustavus Johnson and Elsie Shawe, who planted the seed in 1901. Those pioneers resolutely expected that devotion to the art of music would succeed in

Minnesota. They could, however, hardly have envisioned the trials along the way, the new conditions of life, and the changing musical styles of the twentieth century. The MMTA tree is now full of abundant growth, with a strong trunk of the past, many limbs that have embraced the present, and with new shoots reaching toward the future. MMTA stands as its pioneers did: confident, awaiting the as-yet-unknown challenges of the twenty-first century.

Minnesota Music Teachers Association

Welcome to the Minnesota Music Teachers Association web site.

The Minnesota Music Teachers Association, founded in 1901, is a professional non-profit educational organization and is affiliated with the Music Teachers National Association, founded in 1876. The Minnesota Music Teachers Foundation, founded in 1970, is affiliated with the Minnesota Music Teachers Association.

The mission of the Minnesota Music Teachers Association (MMTA) is to advance the profession of music teaching through education, certification, networking, and advocacy.

Purpose   Products   Links
Programs   Order

The MMTA Web Site

Notes

Chapter 1
Building the Musical Gibraltar

1. The phrase about Gibraltar was used by Willard Patton in Minnesota Music, 1 (1914), p. 9.
2. William H. Leib (1845–1923) of Pennsylvania, tenor, studied in his home state and at Wooster Academy in Ohio. After serving in the Civil War, he studied at the Boston Music School, then resided in the Twin Cities 1875–85, where he taught voice at the State University, conducted many festivals, and sang leading roles in the Gale-Leib Opera Company. Later he taught for 35 years in Kansas City.
3. Charles Henry Morse (1853–1927) of Massachusetts, organist/director, was the first music director of Wellesley College and holder of the first bachelor's degree in music awarded in the U.S. (Boston College). He searched the country for a place to found a conservatory on the model of the New England Conservatory of Music. He chose Minneapolis and opened the Northwestern Conservatory in 1885. He sold it to Clarance Marshall in 1891 for $10,000. While in the Twin Cities he founded and conducted a performing group, the Gounod Club, named after the noted French composer. Just prior to coming to Minnesota, he was one of the founders of the American Guild of Organists, organized in 1884 under the auspices of MTNA. After returning to Boston and New York, he held several organ and college positions.
4. *MTNA Report* (1887), p. 243.
5. Willard Patton (1853–1924) of Maine, tenor/composer, president of MMTA 1887, 1909–1910, before arriving in Minnesota refused an offer to teach at the New England Conservatory, a proposal extended by an initiator of MTNA, Eben Tourjée, the conservatory's founder. Patton (sometimes spelled Patten) was a composer and director as well as a teacher of voice culture. More than any other person, he was the father of MMTA as well as the dean of Minnesota composers. He was particularly active in civic music and directed many organizations including the Filharmonix (1890–1897) and the Philharmonic Club (1898–1901). The Filharmonix was a group of young men interested in music and organized for their own social enjoyment in 1890. In 1891 a male chorus and mandolin club were added and programs by invitation were given. Patton was the first of several directors of this chorus. In 1897 it became a choral society of mixed voices called The

Philharmonic Club. Patton conducted its three concerts each year from 1898 through 1901 when he resigned in order to devote more time to composition. Emil Oberhoffer then took over the conductorship. The club soon found they needed an orchestra to accompany ambitious works. Out of this need, the Minneapolis Symphony was formed in 1903 (this information from the Old Log Book of the Evergreen Club). When Patton became gravely ill in 1924, the community musical leaders arranged a testimonial concert which raised some $1,500, a mark of the esteem in which he was held.

6. *Minneapolis Tribune*, 20 October 1887.

7. *Minneapolis Tribune*, 4 December 1887.

8. Walter Petzet (1866–1941) of Germany, pianist, composer, graduate of the Royal Conservatory at Munich where he was a student of Rheinberger. He was resident at the Northwestern Conservatory in Minneapolis 1887–1890. He then taught piano at the Scharwenka Conservatory in New York before returning to Europe.

9. Carl Lachmund (1857–1928) of Missouri, pianist/violinist, chose the Twin Cities as his residence in 1885 after he returned from study with Franz Liszt (1882–1884). He kept a diary of his lessons and experiences, published as *Living with Liszt*, Franz Liszt Studies Series 4, edited, annotated, and introduced by Alan Walker (Stuyvesant, NY: Pendragon Press, 1995), considered one of the most important sources for understanding the way in which Liszt taught. While in the Twin Cities, he established a youth orchestra, played first violin in a string quartet, and accompanied performers on tour. After the death of his wife, a gifted harpist, he left for New York in 1890 where he founded his own conservatory and formed a Women's String Orchestra.

10. June Drenning Holmquist, "Convention City, The Republicans in Minneapolis, 1892," *Minnesota History* 35 (1956), pp. 64–76.

11. Mrs. K. M. Strong, "The Need of a Recognized Standard," *MTNA Messenger*, 2/2, p. 32.

12. Eugene C. Murdock (1862–1924) of Massachusetts, pianist/composer, president of MMTA 1903–1904, was active in social circles in St. Paul. He wrote a series of songs that were premiered by Christine Miller, the noted mezzo-soprano, who later introduced them to national audiences.

13. Clarance Alden Marshall (1859–1941) of Massachusetts, organist/baritone/composer, president of MMTA 1901–1903, 1906–1907, was educated at Newton High School and then as a special student in art and music at Harvard College. In Boston he was associate conductor of the Handel and Haydn Society, at that time under the leadership of Carl Zerrahn. After leaving Boston, Marshall became music director and organizer of festivals in Saginaw, Nashville and Richmond. He lived in Minneapolis, 1891–1908, after buying the Northwestern Conservatory of Music from Morse. He became head of the Music Department of Stephens College, MO, 1908–1909 where he was soon replaced by an alumnus. He spent his remaining days in Fort Worth, Texas where he never received a position worthy of his training and stature. He grew sick in Fort Worth and retired to Waterville, Maine.

14. Original invitation and *First Annual Report of MMTA* (1902), pp. 49–50.

15. Murdock, "Are We Teaching Music?" *Third Annual Report of MMTA* (1904), p. 29.

16. *First Annual Report of MMTA* (1902), p. 7.

17. Harlow Stearns Gale (1862–1945) of Minneapolis, son of a singing family from New

England, educated at Yale, studied for three years in Leipzig with the founder of modern psychology, Wilhelm Wundt. He taught psychology at the University of Minnesota 1894–1903 where he gave a course linking specific music with psychological factors, evidently the first such course in the world. Gale, an amateur cellist, was stricken with what he called "culture-music" as he found it at Leipzig, Berlin and Bayreuth and returned to be a missionary for music in Minnesota where he organized concerts, wrote notes for the Minneapolis Symphony and was music critic for several newspapers. See Robert T. Laudon's essay, "Gales of Music," on deposit with the Minnesota Historical Society.

18. Franz Kneisel (1865–1926) of Bucharest, violinist/concertmaster of the Boston Symphony, organized the quartet in 1886. The group obtained fame in Europe and the United States. It disbanded in 1917. The quartet had appeared in the Central Presbyterian Church the year before to great acclaim.

19. Robert Griggs Gale (1870–1945) of Minneapolis, pianist/banjoist/teacher/critic/composer, studied in Mineapolis, conducted the Banjo Club of the State University, and then spent 5 years as a student of Hugo Riemann, the noted musical theorist in Leipzig. He returned to Minnesota in 1901 where he and his wife set up a special program for young piano students according to the principles of Riemann. He wrote a column "Chords and Discords" for *The Bellman* from its inception in 1906. He suffered from glaucoma and his poor eyesight forced him to give up music in 1918. He then turned to his other love, the out-of-doors. He became head of the State Fishery at French River on the North Shore of Lake Superior. He retired to California in 1938.

20. The featured performers on this concert program were:

Ella Richards, pianist, who had studied in St. Paul with the New Englander, Charles Graves Titcomb, organist of the People's Church and a prominent piano teacher in St. Paul. She was loaned $425 by the Schubert Club to go to Vienna and study with Leschetizky. Richards became a well-known local soloist and later a correspondent for the *Music News* of Chicago.

Maximilian Leonard Dick, violinist, originally of St. Peter, Minnesota, an outstanding student at St. John's University, Collegeville, Minnesota, later at the Leipzig Conservatory entering in 1887 as Student #4848.

Carlo Fischer, cellist, had studied in Frankfurt am Main under Bernhard Cossman and Hugo Becker, the leading cellists of Germany. He settled permanently in Minneapolis in 1906 as principal cello of the Minneapolis Symphony, and at various times its assistant manager, librarian and program annotator. "One of the best fellows breathing the air of free America. Bohemian all the way through, free of speech, easy of manner, kindly critical, lover of home and fond of the wild" (Old Log Book of the Evergreen Club).

21. See Judith Tick, "Passed Away Is the Piano Girl: Changes in American Musical Life, 1870–1900," *Women Making Music,* ed. Jane Bowers & Judith Tick (Urbana: University of Illinois, 1986), pp. 325–348 and Arthur Loesser, *Men, Women and Pianos* (New York: Simon and Schuster, 1954), pp. 267–283. The Minnesota Federal Census Reports show how much women dominated the musical field. In 1860, out of 630 reported music teachers, only 5 were male—in 1870 only 9 out of 500. At the time of the founding of MMTA female dominance continued but to a lesser degree. These census figures include a large number of public school teachers, then predominantly a woman's profession.

22. See Mary Dillon Foster, *Who's Who among Minnesota Women* (Compiled and published by Mary Dillon Foster, 1924), for information on various clubs and individual women leaders. At least 50 of the women listed in this volume were associated with music. One MMTA President, Wilma Anderson Gilman, wrote a short article on women in music for this publication.

23. David Ferguson Colville (1848–1913) of St. Louis, baritone, president of MMTA 1904–1905, came to St. Paul in 1891 to lead the "quartette" choir of the House of Hope Presbyterian Church, St. Paul. He studied in this country and in England with George Henschel and David Bispham. He taught at Carleton College, Stanley Hall and the Northwestern Conservatory.

24. Hamlin Hunt (1866–1957) of Minnesota, organist, president of MMTA 1910–1911, 1917–1918, was the lone male music graduate (1884) of Carleton College in its early years. He graduated from high school at age 15 and college at age 19. He studied piano with Jedlicska in Berlin, organ with Guilmant in Paris and with Middelschulte in Chicago, all distinguished masters. He was organist/director of Plymouth Congregational Church 1909–1939, organist of the Minneapolis Symphony 1903–1913, and Dean of the MacPhail School of Music for many years. He performed at several world fairs. He was one of 65 selected to play the world's largest organ at St. Louis in 1904. The musical season was really not considered begun in Minneapolis until Hunt played the first of his fall recitals. At these, he introduced Minnesota compositions such as the organ sonatas of J. Victor Bergquist, the "Evening Prayer" of George Fairclough, or "A St. Anne's Fugue" of James Lang, all made by presidents of MMTA. The vespers services at Plymouth Church were preceded by a half-hour organ concert by Hunt.

25. The census figures are a combined aggregate of musicians and music teachers and seem to have been compiled only on the basis of a person's declaration. Thus many grade-school teachers probably reported themselves as "music teachers."

26. John K. Sherman, *Music and Maestros, The Story of the Minneapolis Symphony Orchestra* (Minneapolis: University of Minnesota, 1952), quoting a *Minneapolis Tribune* columnist, pp. 25 and 70.

27. Charles Kunkel (1840–1923) pianist/publisher/composer came to the USA from Germany as one of the Acht-und-vierziger (the 1848ers). He became established in St. Louis, Missouri. Kunkel's *Alpine Storm*, Op. 105 was dedicated to his son, Ludwig Beethoven Kunkel.

28. Oberhoffer and his wife appear in the original list of members; however, as his orchestral duties became greater, he dropped his membership.

29. Sherman, *Music and Maestros,* pp. 70–73 in regard to Oberhoffer's campaign to lift "the city's musical tastes."

30. Harlow Gale, the featured speaker of the first convention, used this term to indicate the distinction between entertainment music, the glees and banjo pieces of his youth, and the serious styles he encountered during his years in Leipzig and Bayreuth.

31. President George Fairclough used this term in his address to the Eighth Convention. For a similar distinction made earlier in Boston, see Michael Broyles, *"Music of the Highest Class," Elitism and Populism in Antebellum Boston* (New Haven: Yale University, 1992).

32. *Eighth Annual Report of MMTA* (1909), p. 4. The second orchestra to which he refers was the St. Paul Symphony Orchestra organized in 1908 under Walter H. Rothwell and active until 1915. After that point, a St. Paul Philharmonic Orchestra under Josef Sainton gave popular concerts.

Chapter 2
America Must Look to the West

1. Gustavus Johnson (1856–1932) of Swedish-English extraction, pianist/composer, president of MMTA 1905–1906, was trained in Stockholm by the best masters in theory, piano, organ, and singing including Mankell, Nordquist, Winge and Håckansson, all teachers at the Royal Conservatory. Johnson did not attend the conservatory but graduated from the Schartau Business College in 1874. He came to the USA in 1875. After a brief stay in Minneapolis, he went to Wisconsin. He returned to Minneapolis in 1880 and remained there until his retirement. During 25 years, he gave many recitals in which he played over 300 different compositions. He was in great demand as an accompanist for such singers as Anna Louise Cary, Kristina Nilson, Lillian Blauvelt and many others. In 1898, he founded the Johnson School of Music, Oratory and Dramatic Art. In the same year, he published *Touch Formation and Elementary Technic for Piano-Forte,* designed to start students on the road to a "musical touch" and to "precede standard works for technical study" especially such fine methods as William Mason's *Touch and Technic.* He was "an unostentatious man, a man with a kindly memory for all of his pupils and for his friends; a man who has always given his best for the advancement of music and a loyalty to the musical growth of this city." (Old Log Book of the Evergreen Club)

   Johnson's sister, Mary Henrietta [Östergren], pianist, was a graduate of the Royal Conservatory in Stockholm. After some residence in Minnesota and Wisconsin, she and her husband settled in Duluth where she became a prominent musician and teacher.

2. The newspapers commented particularly on the second act interior scene which showed a cigar store with a telephone exchange, the latter still a novelty. The libretto of this opera was by Bert W. Ball, the orchestration by J. Bodewaldt Lamp, leader of the Grand Opera House orchestra. The opera had a four-performance run.

3. Olive Fremstad (1871–1951), dramatic soprano, a "love child" adopted by the Fremstad family, a Norwegian father and Swedish mother, came to St. Peter, Minnesota in 1883. She was trained rigorously in music at home and for one year in Minneapolis. After the concert above, she went to New York to study with Bristol, then to Berlin for study with Lilli Lehmann. She sang with extraordinary success in the opera companies of Cologne and Munich as well as many houses of other continental cities. She joined the Metropolitan Opera in 1903 and sang there during the glorious days of Caruso until 1914, and afterwards with other companies until 1920. She was the model for the heroine of Willa Cather's *The Song of the Lark.*

4. See Scot M. Guenter, *The American Flag, 1777–1924* (Cranbury, NJ: Associated University Presses, 1990), Chapter 5, especially pp. 106–109.

5. The organization of the Minnesota Manuscript Club was announced 29 October 1893, its affiliation with the New York Manuscript Society was announced 7 September 1894. The Philadelphia Club began in 1892, Chicago's in 1896.

6. See Robert T. Laudon's Chronology, "Concerts of Minnesota Composers, 1889–1935, and other related events" on deposit in the Research Library of the Minnesota Historical Society.

7. *Minneapolis Tribune,* 3 February 1924, article before the Testimonial Concert. The noted critic and editor, W. S. B. Mathews, came from Chicago to hear the premiere. He wrote a full-scale critique in his magazine *Music: a Monthly Magazine,* 11, p. 581, in which he

discussed each of the movements. He found several deficiencies but concluded that Patton "has performed a serious undertaking and has succeeded remarkably well—Isaiah deserves to go upon the list of honorable undertakings by American composers, the list of which is growing now at a rapid rate."

8. Quoted from *Music: a Monthly Magazine* (June 1899) where W. S. B. Mathews surveys, on pp. 224–227, the work of musical clubs.

9. Ibid., p. 227.

10. W. S. Rockstro, "Oratorio," *A Dictionary of Music and Musicians,* ed. George Grove (Boston: Ditson, 1880) 2, p. 559. See also George P. Upton's *The Standard Oratorios* which traces the history of the oratorio and the early development of sacred music in America.

11. Gerard Tonning (1860–1940) of Norway, choral conductor/composer, studied in Munich with Rheinberger, settled in Duluth in 1887 where he organized choral societies and a chamber music group. He left for Seattle in 1905.

12. Gertrude Sans Souci (original family name, Vel) (1872–1913) of Connecticut, organist/ pianist, came to St. Paul in 1877 where she was educated at St. Joseph's and St. Mary's Academies. She studied music with Charles G. Titcomb and in 1890, she and her sister, Monica, a violinist, went to Berlin where Gertrude studied for 3 years with Oscar Raif and Moritz Moszkowski. Upon her return she became organist of the cathedral in St. Paul and later of Wesley Methodist Church in Minneapolis. She taught at the Northwestern Conservatory of Music. She was one of the few women invited to give organ concerts at the Pan-American Exposition in 1901 at Buffalo, NY, and at the Louisiana Purchase Exposition in 1904 at St. Louis, MO. She became a well-known soloist but perhaps achieved greater fame as a composer of songs. She was correspondent for *The Musical Courier* and for the *St. Paul Globe*. See Robert T. Laudon's essay, "The Dashing Miss Sans Souci," on deposit in the Research Library of the Minnesota Historical Society.

13. Among the previously unidentified principal composers with works on this program are:

Arthur Bergh, violinist, born in St. Paul, 1882, began study in 1887. He went to New York City in 1903 where he was violinist in the New York Symphony Society and the Metropolitan Opera Orchestra, conducted the New York Municipal Concerts in 1911–1914, and served as secretary of the American Music Society.

Claude Madden, violinist, came to the Twin Cities from New York. A brilliant performer who excelled in chamber music, he was violinist of the Minneapolis Symphony in its first three seasons after which he returned to New York.

John Parsons Beach (1887–1953), pianist/composer, studied at the New England Conservatory of Music, came to Minnesota about 1900 and taught at the Northwestern Conservatory. In the season of 1902–1903, he and Emil Oberhoffer were appointed as the first teachers of the University of Minnesota Music Department. He left the cities in 1904.

Carlyle Scott, David Colville, and Marc D. Lombard played important roles in MMTA but were only casual composers.

14. Frances Densmore (1867–1957), probably the most exhaustive researcher in American Indian music and its attendant culture. She seems to have had no connection with MMTA.

15. Arthur Farwell (1872–1952) had some basic training in music in Minnesota and some preliminary education at Baldwin Institute, the predecessor of Macalester College, but he only awakened to a full awareness of music during and after his education at the

Massachusetts Institute of Technology. He studied privately in Boston and then in Germany with Pfitzner and Humperdinck. Entirely devoted to modern American music, he established the Wa-Wan Press (1901–1912) for publication of American works (including songs by MMTA members John Parsons Beach and Stanley Avery). He early cautioned against seeing music "through German spectacles, however wonderful."

16. Stella Stocker (1858–1925) of Illinois, pianist/composer/vocalist studied at the Jacksonville Conservatory. She earned the B.A. from University of Michigan, 1880, came to Duluth in 1885 with her husband, the physician Samuel Marston Stocker. She studied in Paris at the Sorbonne and took vocal lessons with Giovanni Sbiglia. In New York, she studied piano with Xavier Schwarenka and composition with Bruno Oscar Klein. She used Indian melodies in her compositions, themes she collected from the Indians in northern Minnesota where she was known to the Ojibway as O-mes-qua-wi-gi-shi-go-que, Red-sky lady. She was a member of the Chicago and New York Manuscript Societies. In Duluth, she founded an outstanding music study club, The Cecilians, a club still active today. She lectured on the Sbiglia methods of voice production for MMTA. Her daugher, Clara, was also a composer but in a more modern style. She worked a great deal with Finnish folk music and made a melodramatic setting performed at the 1929 MMTA convention of parts of the Kalevala Legend.

17. This story is recounted in the material on Woodruff in the Old Log Book of the Evergreen Club. Henry Seymour Woodruff (1861-1943) of New York State studied for seven years in Cincinnati and later in Paris under Delle Sedie. He was known in the Twin Cities primarily as the conductor of the Apollo Club. According to the Evergreen records: "He is an accompanist of exceptional ability; a gifted whistler which with his improvisations places him in a field by himself; a conscientious teacher of the organ, piano and voice and has been eminently successful in developing artists of international reputation. His instrumental work has necessarily limited his vocal work, although the possessor of a fine baritone voice. A good fellow, well met, always with a word of good cheer on his lips, never a criticism, excepting in rehearsals, and never a slighting remark about a contemporary, and with the desire in his heart to help everyone along the road." See also, Johannes Riedel and Jane Rasmussen Riedel, *Sweeter Than the Honeywell. . . the Apollo Club Male Chorus of Minneapolis, 1895-1995* (Minneapolis: Apollo Club, 1995).

Chapter 3
Help Us All to be Giants

1. Two editions of the *St. Paul and Minneapolis Musicians' Directory* (Minneapolis: National Musicians Directory Company), the *Who's Who in Music and Dramatic Art in the Twin Cities* (Minneapolis: Associated Publicity Bureau, 1925).

2. Carlyle Scott (1873–1945), pianist of Massachusetts, president of MMTA 1907–1908, was raised in Lawrence and Amesbury MA. He received a business education at Lyndon Institute in Vermont. While in the musical town of Lyndonville, he received excellent piano instruction from Mrs. Ranger, the wife of the principal. Therefore, after his graduation in 1891 and an attempt at business, he set off for Leipzig in 1894 where he spent a year at the university and two years at the conservatory. Scott then decided to study privately with

Robert Teichmüller, the young man who was soon to become head of the master class in piano and one of Europe's leading teachers. For a year and a half, Scott was Teichmüller's assistant. While in Leipzig, Scott fell in love with Verna Golden, a violin student from Minneapolis. Upon his return to the USA, the pair set up a music studio and soon married. In 1904, Scott was asked to take over the music work at the University of Minnesota which seemed to be of little consequence to Oberhoffer, the first professor appointed in the season of 1902–1903. Scott single-handedly built a department by teaching all types of music and by supplementing his salary by teaching at the Minneapolis School of Music, Oratory and Dramatic Art. Only in 1913 did he acquire another professor, Donald Ferguson. Gradually the department grew. A new music hall was built in 1922 and more faculty added. Meanwhile his wife was managing the Artist's Series of concerts and the Minneapolis Symphony (after 1930). In recognition of their work, the music building was named Scott Hall. It was the center of many MMTA events for decades.

3. Elam Douglas Bomberger, *The German Musical Training of American Students, 1850–1900* (Doctoral Dissertation, University of Maryland, 1991) is based on surviving conservatory records and personal biographies.

4. The Macalester College Bulletins and the Northwestern Conservatory Bulletins set the European educated apart from those possessing only American education.

5. Thus Donald Ferguson, returned from London, spoke of a musical composition as an "artwork" and his piano teaching as the "dissemination of musical culture" in "The Piano Teacher and the Musical Public," *Proceedings of the Tenth Annual Convention of the Minnesota State Music Teachers' Association* (1911), p. 43.

6. The Minnesota Chapter was only the tenth such unit to be formed in the USA. Personal ties to the British groups existed within MMTA: George Thornton held certificates from the Royal Academy of Music, the Leeds College of Music, and Trinity College in England; Donald Ferguson had studied in London; and George Fairclough had a brother, William, who was a Fellow in the Royal College.

7. George Herbert Fairclough (1869–1954) of Canada, organist/director, president of MMTA 1908–1909, 1918–1919, Fellow in the American Guild of Organists, one of four brilliant sons in a gifted family "could not remember a time when he had not played piano." He held responsible church positions from age 13 on. He studied at the Königliche Hochschule in Berlin, 1893–1895 (one of 15 organ students accepted out of 100 applicants). He came to St. Paul from Kalamazoo College in 1901 to take the posts of organist/director of St. John the Evangelist Episcopal Church and of Mount Zion Hebrew Congregation. He founded the organ programs at Macalester College and the University of Minnesota.

8. George Thornton (1873–1962), organist/director/violinist, president of MMTA 1911–1912, was born in Ireland but had his training in England at Selby Abbey, York Cathedral, Leeds College of Music and the Royal Academy of Music. He was organist/director at Wexford, Ireland, 1893–1906. He came to St. Paul in 1906 and by 1908 held similar posts at St. Clements Episcopal Church (1908–1949) and Mount Zion Temple (1921–1949). Thornton was violinist in the St. Paul Symphony Orchestra and taught violin at Macalester College. He was a faculty member of Hamline University and the MacPhail School of Music.

9. Heinrich Hoevel (1864–1936) of Germany, violinist, president of MMTA 1912–1913,

was educated at the Cologne Conservatory where he studied violin, piano, theory and history. He came to the USA in 1887 and played in various orchestras until 1889 when, after a visit to St. Paul, he decided to locate in the Great Northwest. In the Twin Cities, he played in quartets, the Danz Orchestra, and in the early years of the Minneapolis Symphony. For 17 years he was head of the violin department at the MacPhail School of Music. Like so many Minnesota musicians, he loved the out-of-doors and spent his summers in the "rough country" near Hovland. He willed instruments and furniture to MMTA to help their programs and students. "Heinrich's gentle Deutsche Stimme came in intimate brotherly nearness. It revealed a helpful, generous, kindly, truest gentleman, into whose sympathetic eyes we loved to look as he told us with such quaint and full enthusiasm of the original greatness of Nature and the supernal beauty of an immortal Beethoven quartet." (Eulogy by Harlow Stearns Gale)

10. Willard Patton, "The Examination Plan in Minnesota," *MTNA Proceedings, 1913,* p. 219.

11. Ibid.

12. Ibid., p. 220.

13. Ibid., p. 221.

14. Charles Henry Mills, "The Standardization of Music Teaching," *Official Report of the Eleventh Annual Convention of MMTA,* p. 18.

15. Patton, "Examination Plan," p. 222.

16. Libraries have not conserved *The Western Musical Herald.*

17. Twelve teachers were chosen from among prominent members. Three each for the fields of Piano, Voice/Public School Music, Organ, and Violin began to develop qualifying tests for the Licentiate Certificate. Out of these twelve, one member each was chosen from the fields of Piano, Organ and Voice to formulate the Theory and History questions. All tests were then discussed and approved by the full board

18. Leopold Bruenner (1869–1963) of Germany, organist/director, president of MMTA 1913–1914, was educated in his native Würzburg and later at St. John's University, Minnesota, where he was an honor student. He made the choir at St. Luke's famous in the city. In 1909, he established the St. Paul Choral Art Society of select singers who performed repertory from the Renaissance to Modern Ages. During World War I, Bruenner was the State Director of Liberty Choruses and following the war took over the newly-formed St. Paul Municipal Chorus. He wrote primarily songs and sacred music (including 5 masses).

19. William MacPhail (1881–1962), violinist, president of MMTA 1914–1915, was born in Scotland and arrived in the USA in 1886. He studied violin with Emil Straka, the concermaster of the Danz Orchestra and with Claude Madden. MacPhail played in the second violins for the first year of the Minneapolis Symphony. Then he spent 3 years, 1904–1907, with the most eminent masters in Berlin, Prague and Liège. Upon his return he played many concerts including four times as soloist with the Minneapolis Symphony. In 1907 he began a school for violinists which he transformed into a true conservatory incorporated in 1914. "From a small beginning with the aid of good teachers he has built up a school of music, languages and oratory and the dramatic arts, which with its attendance in 1921 of between four and five thousand students places it in the front rank of American schools." (Old Log Book of the Evergreen Club) In 1923 the present large building of the school was completed and in 1940 a separate College of Music was incorporated as

a nonprofit organization. MacPhail conducted the Minneapolis Shrine Chanters for many years and conducted the Apollo Club, a male chorus, 1928–1950.

20. Harry Phillips (1864–1928) of New York State, baritone, president of MMTA 1915–1916, studied piano, harmony and organ at the Royal Conservatory in Stuttgart, Germany, 1885–1889. He came to St. Paul in 1889 and established himself as a teacher of organ but soon realized that he had an exceptionally fine voice. He then studied vocal culture locally and with masters in centers of the USA and of London, England. He established the Music Department at Macalester College and directed it until his death. He was active as a performer and appeared 4 times with the Minneapolis Symphony. He was in charge of music at Westminister Presbyterian Church in Minneapolis for 22 years and introduced many major choral works to the cities. He was a favorite member of the Evergreen Club and originated its slogan for honoring living musicians: "A rose in the hand is worth two on the grave."

21. J. Austin Williams (b. 1876) of England, tenor/director, president of MMTA 1916–1917, was born in Gloucestershire. He came to Minneapolis in 1897 convinced that there were opportunities for business and art. He gave up his rope business and entered an active musical career in 1902. He studied in America and Europe with well-known voice teachers. He was one of the first to take the certification examinations of MMTA and passed with high marks. He served as director for a number of churches but his main service was with Wesley Methodist Church, 1923–1949, where he conducted 10 light operas with the young people as part of the church's Lyceum Course.

22. Patton, "Examination Plan," p. 227.

23. Donald Ferguson, "Report of Committee for Standardized Course," *Music News* (Chicago), 3 July 1917, p. 20.

Chapter 4
To Issue Certificates of Proficiency

1. MMTA Articles of Incorporation

2. *Minnesota Music,* 1/6 (November 1914), p. 4.

3. The "Recommendations as to the Scope and Character of the Various Examinations," in the appendix to the constitution adopted after incorporation, outlines the general principles and states that the advanced examinations should "conform to the standards set by the examinations given in 1911 for Associateship and Fellowship in the American Guild of Organists: the difference being recognized that the examinations of MMTA are examinations for teachers, not for executants."

Chapter 5
The Most Important Era

1. "Minnesota Teachers Hail New Musical Era," *Musical America* (5 July 1919), p. 35. The convention was also reported in *Music News* [Chicago], 4 July 1919, pp. 17–23.

2. During the conflict the country realized that it still had many residents with close ties to the "old country" and had many new immigrants who had yet to learn American ways. To achieve a unity seemed necessary in wartime and desirable in peacetime. A large movement of Americanization arose and persisted into the post-war years. The University of Minnesota even had Americanization professors and a four-year Bachelor of Science Program in Americanization Training.

3. Program of the Music Week preserved in the St. Paul Public Library Music Department files.

4. Kenneth S. Clark, *Municipal Aid to Music in America* (New York: National Bureau for the Advancement of Music, 1925), p. 202.

5. James Lang's address as President of MMTA at the 19th Convention in 1920.

6. The local colleges and universities were not equipped in faculty or instruments to teach "photo-playing." Fairclough, at Macalester College and the University of Minnesota, found a tremendous increase in enrollment but continued to teach only church and concert playing. The MacPhail School, on the other hand, installed a "Wurlitzer orchestral, three manual organ of the latest type" and established a Theatre Organ Department under the leadership of Eddy Dunstedter, the organist of the State Theater in Minneapolis.

7. The one played by MMTA members, Hamlin Hunt, Gertrude Sans Souci and George Fairclough in 1904.

8. See Kenneth S. Clark, *Music in Industry* (New York: National Bureau for the Advancement of Music, 1929), pp. 346–347. See also Linda L. Tyler, "Commerce and Poetry Hand in Hand, Music in American Department Stores, 1880–1930," *Journal of the American Musicological Society,* 45 (1992), pp. 75–120.

9. Clark, *Music in Industry,* pp. 287–293, gives a partial listing of Minnesota groups. The Great Northern Choruses were led by MMTA president, George Thornton.

10. On the national scene, the Juilliard and Curtis schools opened in 1924.

11. *Bulletin of the Minneapolis School of Music,* 1919–1920, p. 8.

12. By 1926–1927, the catalogue indicated these numbers.

13. *Civic and Commerce Bulletin* (May, 1926), quoting *The Musical Courier* of 7 January 1926.

14. The building (now named Scott Hall) was cited as one of the most important examples in Charles Z. Klauder and Herbert C. Wise, *College Architecture in America* (New York: Charles Scribner's Sons, 1929), p. 206 f. It was designed to avoid that "strange irony of fate" in which "the arts devoted to the beautiful should be housed in ugly buildings." One approached it with appropriate awe by broad steps leading up to the entrance. The lobby had beautiful wall-tiles showing Renaissance musicians. The library furnishings were chosen by the president of the Handicraft Guild, Mrs. Charles A. Bovey.

15. Information on James Lang is scanty. He evidently was educated in London. In the Twin Cities, he was organist of Hamline Methodist Church and the Jewish Reform Synagogue.

16. Elsie M. Shawe (1866–1962), contralto/organist/public school musician, president of MMTA, 1920–1921 came of a musical family. Her mother had been associated with music at St. Mary's Catholic Church in St. Paul and Shawe became director at the church. Her annual concerts were eagerly anticipated and attended. She became president of the Schubert Club, 1900–1902, and had directed their women's chorus prior to that. In

1897–1898, she was appointed Supervisor of Music in the St. Paul Public Schools, a position she held until her retirement in 1933.

17. Stanley R. Avery (1879–1967) of New York, organist/choir master/composer, president of MMTA 1921–1922 was born in Yonkers and had his early education there. He began composing at an early age. After study with several well-known organists and while still a student in high school, he became organist of Saint Andrew's Episcopal Church in Yonkers. After high school, he studied music at Columbia College where he had some work with MacDowell. Later he spent a brief time in Europe studying with Hans Pfitzner and Engelbert Humperdinck. He was called to St. Mark's Church in Minneapolis where he served from 1910 to 1950. In 1919, he was appointed head of a new department for church music, choir directing and chorus singing at the MacPhail School, a position he held until 1966. Avery wrote a large quantity of music, songs, operettas, sacred music, organ and piano compositions, a significant number of which were published.

18. As hostilities of World War I ceased, France showed her gratitude for the American Expeditionary Forces in a musical way. As a token of the nation's appreciation, she established in 1921 the American Conservatory at Fontainebleau, which rapidly became a cradle for American composers. In addition, she sent her premier orchestra, that of the Concerts du Conservatoire, on a tour of the States. In New York, E. Robert Schmitz, the French pianist, organized a Franco-American Musical Society—later called Pro-Musica—with branches throughout the country pledged to promote new music. The Minneapolis Chapter was organized in 1924 and soon reached a membership of 130. Such actions tempered the large influence that German music had upon the country and presented new challenges to the older generations.

19. R. Buchanon Morton (1876–1946) of Scotland, organist/director/vocal teacher, president of MMTA 1922–1924, was reared in his native land. His advanced studies were at the Dresden Conservatory of Music, 1898–1901 where he worked with some of the best German masters including: in piano, Rappoldi-Kahrer, a student of Liszt, and in theory, Felix Draeseke, an ardent Wagnerian. Upon his return to Scotland, he obtained his professional diplomas. He came to the USA in 1914 and became organist-choirmaster in the Glen Avon Presbyterian Church in Duluth. In 1917, he was appointed to a similar position at the House of Hope Presbyterian Church in St. Paul. In 1925 he became carillonneur of the church. Gradually the teaching of voice became his major area. He was one of the first to use phonograph recordings of students.

20. During his years in Scotland, Morton had been president of the Aberdeen Music Teachers Association and a member of the Incorporated Society of Musicians. In Duluth he had founded the Duluth Music Teachers Association. In the Twin Cities he served as Dean of the Minnesota Chapter of the American Guild of Organists. Such background fitted him well for his MMTA post.

21. The artist-members presented on this recital were:

Eleanor Poehler (?–1949), soprano, who studied three years with Anna Schoen-René and three years with Oscar Seagle and Charles Bowes in New York City and England. She taught voice at the MacPhail School and at Miss Woods Kindergarten School. She was entertainment manager of the Institute of Arts and manager of the Minneapolis String Quartet.

Harrison Wall Johnson (1881–1945), born in southern Minnesota, who studied in Minneapolis and then in Berlin with Busoni. He taught regularly at the MacPhail School, for short periods of time at the University of Minnesota, and from 1933 to 1943 at the Academy of Allied Arts in New York City. He gave numerous recitals and played the local premiere of Gershwin's *Rhapsody in Blue* with the Minneapolis Symphony.

Louise Chapman, who later compiled an important chronology of musical events, "The First Fifty Years of Music in Minneapolis, 1850–1900," based upon newspaper accounts (on deposit in the Minneapolis Room, Special Collections, of the Minneapolis Public Library).

22. Donald Nivison Ferguson (1882–1985), pianist/composer/historian, president of MMTA, 1924–1927, was born in Waupan, Wisconsin. He graduated from the University of Wisconsin in 1904 (Major in French) and then went to London for four years of study with Michael Hambourg in piano and Josef Holbrooke in composition. He came to Minneapolis in 1909 where he taught privately until 1913 when he joined the staff of the University of Minnesota (the second teacher of the department). For his students, he wrote *A History of Musical Thought,* one of the earliest widely-accepted histories. He earned the M.A. in French from the Univ. of Minnesota in 1922 (his hobby was languages, especially Latin) and spent the year of 1929–1930 studying music at the University of Vienna. He formed a Bach Society in 1932, a group which performed for MMTA several times and which he conducted until 1950. He wrote the program notes for the concerts of the Minneapolis Symphony, 1930–1960. He retired from his university position in 1950 and became professor at Macalester College for the next eleven years. His greatest interest was in the psychological basis of musical expression, a topic which he considered in numerous publications. He became affectionately known as "Fergie" to generations of musicians and students. In recognition of his contributions, the building of the University of Minnesota School of Music was named Ferguson Hall.

23. Ferguson, "How Can Music Express Emotion," *Papers and Proceedings of the Music Teachers National Association,* 20 (1925), p. 32.

24. *Papers and Proceedings of the Music Teachers National Association,* 22 (1927), (Hartford, Conn.: The Association, 1928), p. 21. William Arms Fisher (1861–1948) had studied theory with Horatio Parker and singing with William Shakespeare. He became editor and publisher for Oliver Ditson & Company. He wrote the words *Goin' Home* to the slow movement of the New World Symphony.

25. Marshall's harsh words on Texas are the result of his own difficulties in getting established in Fort Worth coupled with the fact that Texas had nothing to match the triumphant tours of the Minneapolis Symphony to that region.

26. Sponsored by the Public School Music League.

27. Sponsored by the Minnesota Bandmasters Association.

28. J. Victor Bergquist (1877–1935) of Swedish ancestry, organist/composer, president of MMTA 1927–1929, was born in St. Peter, Minnesota. He attended Gustavus Adolphus College in St. Peter where he obtained his Bachelor of Music with honors in 3 years, 1895 (age 18). He was organist of Augustana Lutheran Church, Minneapolis, through 1899 and studied with leading teachers in the city. He entered the Berlin Conservatory in 1900 where he studied organ with Grunicke, composition with Wilhelm Berger and piano with

Scharwenka. In 1902 he moved to Paris to study with Guilmant for a year. In 1903, he started an active music program at Augustana Church. In 1912–1918, he became conductor of the Handel Oratorio Society and head of the Music Conservatory of Åugustana College, Rock Island, Illinois. In 1918 he returned to Minneapolis where he became organist/director of Central Lutheran Church, teacher of organ, piano and composition at the MacPhail School, and director of the music credit system in the Minneapolis Public High Schools where he held yearly festivals of music by high school composers who during his tenure produced some 1200 compositions. Besides his compositions, he published one book, *Theory of Self Expression in Music.*

29. President's address by J. Victor Bergquist, 17 May 1928, Hotel Radisson, Minneapolis, "One of our neighboring state associations has gone on the rocks and disbanded after more than thirty years' existence. I believe they lost sight of the fact that they were a teachers' organization."

30. The *Northwest Musical Herald* began publication in November of 1926 under the editorship of the pianist, Gabriel Fenyves, and with an advisory group including the music critics of the Twin Cities as well as the president of MMTA. It is a rich source of information up into the first years of the Great Depression at which point it gradually declined until its demise in the spring of 1934.

31. President's address by J. Victor Bergquist, 17 May 1928, Hotel Radisson, Minneapolis.

32. Ibid.

33. President's address by Donald Ferguson, 17 June 1926, St. Paul Hotel.

Chapter 6
A Workable Procedure

1. Harry M. Lokken, *Growth and Accessibility of Public High Schools, in Minnesota,* Master's Thesis University of Minnesota (1932), pp. 56–57.

2. Dyer Brothers in St. Paul maintained through the 1930s a Saturday youth band conducted by Ernest Whitbecker. It played for civic occasions.

3. Will Earhart, *Music in the Public Schools* (Washington: Govt. Printing Office, 1914), p. 44.

4. Will Earhart & Osbourne McConathy, *Music in Secondary Schools* (Washington: Govt. Printing Office, 1918), p. 28.

5. This was the date of the pilot course at West High School; all five high schools adopted the procedure the following year.

6. Thaddeus P. Giddings (1868–1954), public school musician, was born in Anoka, Minnesota. He had three summer sessions at the Western Normal Music School but was largely self-taught. He was Supervisor of Music of the Moline, Illinois Schools, 1891–1894, Oak Park, Illinois Schools, 1894–1910, and of the Minneapolis Schools, 1910–1942. He held the associate certificate in MMTA. He was widely known as a music reading specialist. He taught Public School Music at the MacPhail School, 1923–1942 and was co-founder of the National Music Camp at Interlochen, Michigan. See Charles M. McDermid, *Thaddeus P. Giddings: A Biography* (Ann Arbor: University of Michigan Doctoral Dissertation, 1967).

7. Gertrude Ann Dobyns (1877–1973), pianist, composer and teacher was born in Shelbyville and raised in Shelbina, Missouri. She studied with private teachers in the USA and then spent four years in Germany. She was a student at the Stern Conservatory (Berlin): piano with Ernst Jedliczka (pupil of Tschaikowsky and Rubenstein), musical theory with Ludwig Bussler and at the Dresden Conservatory: piano with Bertrand Roth (pupil of Liszt), musical theory with W. Albert Rischbieter. She came in 1901 to Minneapolis where she taught privately, at Stanley Hall and at the Northwestern Conservatory. Her concerts in Germany and the USA earned her rave reviews. She gave special lectures on the Minneapolis symphony repertory before concerts and had her students study the masterworks in orchestral literature. In the time of World War I, she went to France as a volunteer member of the first foreign service entertainment group sent abroad. Following the war, she returned to Shelbina where she built a music studio and guided generations of students in art and music while she became a community leader in civic affairs. Her songs were performed at the 1910 convention of MMTA.

8. Minneapolis Notes," *Music News* (Chicago), 31 May 1918, pp. 28–29.

9. "An Unusual Musical Development in Minneapolis," *Music News* (Chicago), 4 July 1919, p. 23.

10. At various times, Paul Oberg, the Chairman of the Music and Music Education Departments of the University of Minnesota, and Eunice Norton, the most renowned piano soloist Minnesota has produced, began their careers in this program.

11. McDermid, *Thaddeus P. Giddings*, pp. 173–179.

12. Charles Edward Russell, *The American Orchestra and Theodore Thomas* (Garden City: Doubleday, Page, 1927), p. 310, based on a special report of Ruth Anderson.

13. Mankato had a similar system and Donald Ferguson went to judge their accomplishments at the end of the year.

14. J. Victor Bergquist, Report at the 1924 Convention, from the stenographic record of the proceedings, pp. 6–15, MMTA Papers, Minnesota Historical Society.

15. *Minutes of the State Board of Education* (1924–1925), p. 160.

16. State of Minnesota, Department of Education, *The High School Curriculum and Syllabi of High School Subjects* (June, 1925).

17. Ibid., Bulletin #1, Introduction, p. 10. One might contrast this with the subject of "Art" which as a Constant received a whole syllabus. Art however was conceived of as a grand combination of fine and useful arts. Music evidently was considered not useful and perhaps not "fine" either.

18. Ibid., pp. 42–44.

19. Though MMTA tried for a number of years afterward to establish a system to give credit to hard-working students, the attitude of central administration never changed. At a meeting of 15 December 1933, the Board reaffirmed its earlier action in response to another presentation by MMTA. Minneapolis, as a city of the first class, continued its program, but even there, the program gradually faded away. Bergquist died in 1935; Giddings retired in 1942. This fading of the "old guard," the impact of the Depression and World War II, conspired against the Minneapolis Plan.

Chapter 7
The Present Era of Enforced Leisure

1. *Northwest Musical Herald,* 8/3 (September-October 1933), p. 2.
2. *Northwest Musical Herald,* 8/3 (September-October 1933), p. 3.
3. C. Wesley Anderson, "Problem of Unemployment," *Northwest Musical Herald,* 4/8 (May 1930), p. 6.
4. Sherman, *Music and Maestros,* pp. 206–209 tells the story of the bleakest days.
5. Sister Ann Thomasine Sampson, "St. Agatha's Conservatory and the Pursuit of Excellence," *Ramsey County History,* 24/1, pp. 10–11.
6. Ethel Hascall, "Musical Memories: Madeleine (Ravenscroft) Titus," *MMTA Newsletter* (February 1991), p. 7. This is one of a series of Heritage Vignettes collected by Ethel Hascall as part of the preparation for the MMTA Centennial.
7. Don W. Larson, *Land of the Giants, A History of Minnesota Business* (Minneapolis: Dorn Books, 1979), p. 142.
8. Ibid., p. 137.
9. In 1940, unemployment was still over 14%.
10. Marvin S. Thostenson, A History of the First Century of the Iowa Music Teachers Association, *1885–1985* (Iowa Music Teachers Association, 1985), pp. 38–40.
11. Carl A. Jensen (1886–1973) of Danish ancestry, pianist/organist/composer/teacher, president of MMTA 1929–1931, 1944–1947, studied piano with James A. Bliss and organ with Hamlin Hunt. He first prepared for a career in law and then began his professional musical career in Minneapolis in 1913. He held the Associate Degree in the American Guild of Organists (1924) and served as organist/director of Plymouth Church and Macalester Presbyterian Church in St. Paul and of Temple Israel in Minneapolis. He joined the Macalester Conservatory in 1925 as head of the department of musical theory and became director of the conservatory in 1928 until his retirement in 1956. He held the Associate Certificate in MMTA (1923). In Toronto in 1942, he passed an examination conducted by Healy Willan (noted Canadian organist/composer) and was awarded the Licentiate degree of Trinity College of Music (London, England). Jensen was particularly interested in contemporary music and was a friend of John Becker, the avant-garde composer. Mrs. Becker remembers him as "a good, gentle, kind man." Macalester College has a complete file on Jensen in its archives.
12. Harry W. Ranks, organist/director/public school musician, president of MMTA, 1931–1934, graduated from the Yale University School of Music (took two years of post-graduate work there) and from the Northampton Institute of Music Pedagogy. He was head of the Music Department of the New Britain (Connecticut) State Normal School, 1914–1920. He then came to Minneapolis where he became organist/director of the Church of the Redeemer and director of the Scottish Rite Choir. He taught at Minnesota College and the Minneapolis College of Music. He was Coordinator of Applied Music in the Minneapolis Public Schools and took over the high school instruction, contest and yearly concerts of young composers in 1935. He published *Composing Your Own Music* (1939).
13. John G. Hinderer, "To Keep Music Teaching Free from Governmental Interference," *The*

Musician, May, 1929, p. 30. Hinderer (1885–1963), St. Paul pianist/teacher, was a telegraph operator who studied locally and then for short periods with Breithaupt, Matthay, and Godowsky. He had an uncanny knack for organizing knowledge and developed a whole method from these short studies. He was so opposed to anything smacking of governmental control that he even set up his own organization, the American Guild of Music Teachers which evidently, despite its title, remained a local group. His most extensive musical connection was with Leopold Godowsky for whom he served for many years as a sort of secretary. Hinderer saved almost all of his own papers and those of the Guild. They are on deposit in the Minnesota Historical Society Research Library. Through his connection with Friedheim, a Liszt pupil, he traced his musical "genealogy" back to Beethoven, Haydn, Bach, and ultimately to Binchois! He had intended to write a biography of Godowsky but had not finished it before his death by suicide (due to back pain and troubles with income tax in regard to his compositions).

14. Editorial, *The Bandmaster,* 1928, p. 18.

15. William Wellington Norton was granted the A.B. in 1909 and the A.M. in 1910 (the latter with a thesis, "The Discrimination of Pitch and its Relation to Tonality") by the University of Minnesota. He assembled *The University of Minnesota Song Book* (1911). Ever the organizer, he founded The Musical Federation of the university joining the Euterpean Club, orchestra, glee club, mandolin club and band "to promote all musical interests . . . provide Thursday music in chapel, to assist in building up a college of music." He taught at the University of North Dakota at Grand Forks, conducted Community Sings during the First World War, and eventually took the position in community music at Flint, Michigan.

16. William Norton, "The Kaleidoscopic View," *Yearbook of the Music Supervisors National Conference,* 26 (1933), pp. 54–55. The prevailing view of the educators coincided in large part with the philosophy of John Dewey, a view that was sweeping educational circles at this period. Dewey's influential *Art as Experience* in which he maintained that art existed for the enhancement of life was published in 1934, the year following the crucial last convention of the Music Supervisors. His pragmatic ideas however had been tested in laboratory schools and had been presented in numerous publications prior to 1934.

17. The phrase comes from the *Federal Music Project Manual,* evidently written primarily by famed conductor, Nicolai Sokoloff, director of the project. There was a strong element of music appreciation and democratization of music in the project. See Cornelius B. Canon, *The Federal Music Project of the Works Progress Administration: Music in a Democracy* (Dissertation, University of Minnesota, 1963).

18. Glenn Dillard Gunn, "Music in the Public Schools and the Professional Teachers," *Yearbook of the Music Supervisors National Conference,* 26 (1933), p. 56.

Chapter 8
I Admire Your Work and Aims

1. Percy Grainger to Wilma Anderson; England, 27 October 1936.

2. Harriett Gold Allen (1890–1970), pianist, president of MMTA 1934–1935, studied with

E. C. Murdock, second president of MMTA, and Carlyle Scott, fifth president of MMTA. In 1910, she received the Certificate of Proficiency in piano and harmony at the University of Minnesota in a period before music degrees were granted. Eager to progress, she spent summers studying: in England with Tobias Matthay (1929) and at Chautauqua with Ernest Hutchinson. She spent 8 months in New York City studying technique with Abby Whiteside. Allen taught at the MacPhail School and was organist of several churches. She was on the faculty of Hamline University 1926–1937 and the faculty of Macalester College, 1938–1951. Eunice Norton, the most famous pianist Minnesota has produced, was her student.

3. The Wadena group kept excellent records and so we can recount their actions in more detail than in other places where few records were kept.

4. This town, more enterprising than some, was already supporting a concert series which was to feature in that year the Minneapolis Symphony, the Princess Pat Band (from Canada), and the St. Olaf Choir.

5. Wilma Anderson Gilman (1881–1971), pianist, president of MMTA, 1935–1937, was a student of Arthur Van Dooren in Brussels, toured as soloist and accompanist 1900–1907, joined Giddings in his Minneapolis school work to offer piano lessons, taught for many years at the MacPhail School, active in the Thursday Musical, Phi Beta (the honorary music fraternity), State Federation of Music Clubs, and the National Music Camp in addition to MMTA. Her husband Charles and she lived an outdoor life during the summers. Her daughter, Francis, is a noted harpist in the Twin Cities, and her granddaughter, Lynn, a harpist and administrator in the School of Music of the University of Michigan.

6. Taped recollections of Gilman gathered and transcribed as *Remembrances* by Grieg Aspnes, her son-in-law. Piano ensembles were popular during the 19th and early 20th centuries, a time when recordings were not available and concerts in small centers were rare. Mrs. Gilman may also have been aware of earlier Ten-Piano Concerts conducted by Henri Verbrugghen, the second conductor of the Minneapolis Symphony in April of 1928. See Robert T. Laudon, "How the Ten-Piano Contest Started" in *MMTA Newsletter*, February 1994, p. 7.

7. *The Minneapolis Star,* 30 December 1936.

8. At least one of his compositions, especially the popular *Shepherd's Hey, Country Gardens,* or *Molly on the Shore* as well as more complex pieces had been played each year in the preceding two decades by the Minneapolis Symphony. Nearly every piano student of the era hoped to play *Country Gardens.*

9. Lenore Engdahl to Russell Harris, 21 March 1985. Lenore Engdahl was a fine pianist who made a well-received recording of the music of Griffes. Later she moved to Massachusetts.

10. Chester E. Campbell, violinist, president of MMTA, 1937-1938, studied with George Klass of Minneapolis; then after service in the infantry in World War I, with Fernand Carles, Noël Ciasso, and Emile Joy at the Montpellier Conservatory in France. Upon return to the USA, Campbell briefly played viola in the Minneapolis Symphony and then taught at St. Thomas College, Cretin High School, and Visitation Convent in St. Paul. He directed the orchestra and band of Central High School in St. Paul and the MacPhail Orchestral Art Society in Minneapolis in addition to studio lessons at the MacPhail School. His wife, Elsie Wolfe Campbell, was a well-known pianist and teacher in the area.

11. Agnes Rast Snyder (1895-1961), contralto, president of MMTA 1938-1944, was born at

Red Wing, Minnesota, the daughter of the Reverend Gustaf Rast and Johanna Anderson Rast. She first studied piano but when the family moved to Minneapolis in 1910, friends commented on her beautiful voice. She studied singing locally from 1912 through 1918. Beginning in 1919, she spent a year and a half in Wiesbaden, Germany, studying with Rudolph Weyrauch of the opera there. Upon her return, she taught at Minnesota College and from 1927 through 1945 at the University of Minnesota. She possessed a powerful but graceful voice coupled with superb musicianship. so that she was much in demand as a soloist and oratorio performer. She had an extensive repertory and performed many compositions of Minnesotans. Her sister, Laurinda, was an organist and choir director.

12. The United States society was still the umbrella organization for various musical interests but was beginning to splinter into special groups: the Music Library Association had been founded in 1931, the Music Educator's National Conference and the American Musicological Society in 1934. As yet, however, specialists of all sorts including these groups continued to come to MTNA conventions where they presented a great variety of topics.

13. A smaller convention was mounted for the year 1944 in Cincinnati. During the other war years, the executive committee continued to meet and committee reports were issued together with a few papers that had been sent by mail. In 1943, for the first time since the formation of MTNA the annual report was not issued.

14. The importance of local developments in the modern style was recognized by Roger Sessions, one of the leaders of the movement. In a letter to Ernst Krenek, 6 December 1947, *The Correspondence of Roger Sessions*, ed. Audrey Olmstead, (Boston: Northeastern University Press, 1992), Sessions, after a visit to Minneapolis to hear his violin concerto, wrote: "I was also very much impressed by the activity for Contemporary music that goes on there" and expressed his conviction that "this region and the 'Twin Cities seem to me the most hopeful places" for music in the U.S.

15. Report of Carl A. Jensen in *MTNA Proceedings* (1946), p. 414.

16. Robert N. Pearson, pianist, president of MMTA 1947–1948, taught at the MacPhail School and Minnehaha Academy.

Chapter 9
We are Growing

1. Paul Matthews Oberg (1904–1988), pianist/organist, president of MMTA 1948–1952, was educated in the Minneapolis High Schools in their theory and composition program, at the University of Minnesota where he received his bachelor's degree *magna cum laude* in 1925, at the Juilliard School, and later at the Eastman School of Music where he received a Master's degree in 1939 and Doctoral degree in 1944. He served as staff pianist and organist for WCCO (a remarkable sight reader), organist for several churches and for the Minneapolis Symphony. He taught at the University of Wichita, Kansas, 1933–1942. In 1942 he was appointed Professor and Chairman of the Departments of Music and Music Education of the University of Minnesota. He retired in 1972 but continued to play organ for two churches in San Diego, his retirement home.

2. See Chapter 1 of Michael J. Bennett's *When Dreams Came True, The GI Bill and the Making of Modern America* (Washington: Brassey's, 1996).

3. A materials committee was appointed each year to handle the piano lists. Other groups had to compile lists for voice, organ, violin and woodwind contestants.

4. From the list for 1965.

5. Ibid.

6. Ibid.

7. Markley, the longest-serving Contest Chairman (1959–1975 plus a year of transition) spoke of the "immensity of the project" in her report on the 50th Anniversary of the concert, 1 June 1985. Gladys Markley studied piano privately with a tutor/governess, piano and music education at the University of Kansas, taught briefly in a public school and then privately in St. Paul for many years.

8. While the Schmitt Company provided pianos for the longest period of time, several other firms, Bodine Piano, Thorgaard-Anderson Piano, and Lind Music, helped in the early years.

9. Dora Gosso, pianist, president of MMTA 1952–1955, was at the time of her presidency teaching at Concordia College in St. Paul.

10. Russell G. Harris (1914–1995), pianist/composer, president of MMTA 1955–1956, 1983–1985, received his B.Mus. degree from Knox College (Phi Beta Kappa) and M.Mus. degree from the University of Michigan. He studied later with numerous distinguished composers. He taught first at Baylor University and then at Hamline University (1943–1979, head of department, 1948–1971). Harris was a long-time member and tireless worker for MMTA and a member of MTNA from 1936 to his death.

11. From 1955 through 1969, MTNA held conventions only biennially. During this period the regional conventions became especially important.

12. Class piano lessons were becoming popular at this time and their teachers used theory nomenclature and sound to establish communication among their young musicians. A number of commercial publishers had begun putting out theory worksheets. The Canadian system of syllabi and tests supervised by the Toronto Conservatory and the University of Manitoba were beginning to be known in Minnesota.

13. The members of this forum were Russell Harris of Hamline University, Glen Glasow of the College of Saint Catherine, Martha Baker of the MacPhail College of Music, and Arthur Campbell of St. Olaf College. At the June convention in 1954, George chaired a forum, "The Music Composer Looks at Teaching Music." Unfortunately George left the state soon after this forum and before any official action had been taken by MMTA.

14. *The Minnesota Daily,* 15 May 1961.

15. Louise Guhl, *Odyssey of a Small Town Piano Teacher,* (San Diego: Neil A Kjos, 1994), p.15.

16. Donald Anderson, studied piano and composition with Professor Karl Wolff in Fort Frances, Ontario, received a B.S. in music and a M.S. in Music Education at the University of Minnesota. He had a postgraduate semester at Columbia University. He taught Junior and Senior High School Music at Dassel, Minnesota, High School Band and Orchestra at Dubuque, Iowa. The greater portion of his professional life was spent as as an independent piano teacher and tuner, 1949–1979, at Fosston and Crookston, Minnesota. He helped establish the Northwest District of MMTA, gave workshops on composing, and served on the theory committee.

17. In "Meeting with the Composer," *Celebrating Women of Excellence through Music* (Minneapolis: The Upper Midwest Women's History Center, 1998), p. 12.

18. Robert T. Laudon, pianist/musicologist, president of MMTA 1961–1963, studied piano with Earl Rymer and Donald Ferguson at the University of Minnesota (1940–42, 1946–50) where he received the B.A. *magna cum laude* (1947, Phi Beta Kappa), and the M.A. in music history (1950). Later he received the Ph.D. in musicology at the University of Illinois, (1969). He served in the Army Air Corps (1942–1946), taught at St. Thomas College (1950–52), Jamestown College (1952–1955), St. Cloud State College (1955–1961), and the University of Minnesota (1962–1986).

19. Louise [Peterson] Guhl, pianist, president of MMTA 1971– 1973, daughter of a soprano who named her after Louise Homer, the famous singer, studied at St. Olaf College (B.A. 1929), in Berlin with Franz Xaver Muehlbauer (1936–1937), and in the U.S. with Guy Maier and Bernhard Weiser. She taught privately and was associate professor of piano pedagogy and class piano at the University of Minnesota (1967–1976) using her text, *Keyboard Proficiency* (Barnes and Noble). Author of *The Magic Reader*, books 1–5, *Sight Read Successfully*, books 1–3, and *Odyssey of a Small Town Piano Teacher*.

20. There was a brief but unsuccessful attempt in 1953 to resuscitate the old licentiate test.

21. Roy A. Schuessler (1910–1982), baritone/vocal diagnostician/authority on the adolescent voice, president of MMTA 1963–1965, studied at the University of Wichita (B.A. 1932) and Northwestern University (M.M. 1938). He was choral director of the prestigious Evanston Township High School (Illinois, 1936–1943). He served in the US Navy (1943–1946), taught voice at University of Minnesota (1946–1980) and became head of the music department (1965–1975).

22. Smith and MacPhail were directors of the leading conservatories of Minneapolis.

23. Anthony L.Chiuminatto (1904–1973), came to the U.S. from Turin, Italy, in 1904, studied at the Green Bay Business College, Milwaukee Conservatory of Music and later studied violin, musicology and romance languages at the University of Turin where he received his B.A. He spent 4 years at the Verdi Royal Conservatory. He received the B.Mus. and M.Mus. from the Chicago Conservatory of Music (1929), the B.Mus.Ed. (1939), M.Mus.Ed (1941) and Ph.D. in musicology (1959) from Northwestern University. He taught in Chicago at the Columbia School of Music. Later he taught at the University of Wichita and then became Chairman of the Department of Music at St. Thomas College. He served in World War II as interpreter in Africa and Europe. "Tony," as he was affectionately known, served as chairman of the certification committee and handled the national accreditation program for MMTA.

24. John Thut (1898–1994), tenor/choir director, president of MMTA 1958–1961, studied at Goshen Collge, (A.B. 1923), the American Conservatory of Music, Chicago, (B.Mus. 1929, M.Mus. 1936). He taught at Luther Institute, Chicago (1934–1944) and Augsburg College, Minneapolis (1947–1966). He held various offices including national secretary in the National Association of Teachers of Singing (NATS) of which he had been a charter member in 1944.

25. MMTA Report of the President, 24 June 1957.

26. Aaron Copland, *What to Listen for in Music* (New York: McGraw-Hill, 1957), p. 249.

Chapter 10
A New Way of Life—The Syllabus Arrives

1. The phrase was used by Sister Mary Davida Wood in a newsletter of 1975. She could contemplate such changes from the standpoint of some 40 years membership in MMTA.

2. Paul Freed, pianist, president of MMTA 1967–1969, studied from age 11 to 18 with Alma Mehus Studness (student of Adele aus der Ohe, Moritz Rosenthal and Josef Lhevinne) and Lenore Cunningham (student of Frank Mannheimer). He earned the B.A. at Hamline University, Soloist Diploma at the Basel Conservatory (with Paul Baumgartner) and the M.M. at Florida State University (with Ernst von Dohnanyi). He taught undergraduate and graduate piano and piano literature at the University of Minnesota where he supervised the training of advanced students.

3. At the 1969 convention.

4. College teachers were not only concerned with prospective piano majors but also with voice and instrumental students who needed piano skills.

5. Shirley Rediger, piano teacher/arts leader, president of MMTA 1969–1971, found her performing and teaching cut short by a serious auto accident. After that, she earned a Masters Degree in Arts Management at the University of Wisconsin-Madison. She helped develop the Wisconsin Youth Symphony, Wisconsin Ballet Company, the Madison Civic Repertory Theatre, fourteen heritage/cultural arts centers in Alaska, and similar work in Guam, Saipan, American Samoa and in California. When she died in 1988, she was at work on projects in Detroit and in Australia.

6. Ethel Hascall, pianist/piano teacher, received the B.Mus. degree with honors from St. Olaf College. She taught briefly in the public schools and then for forty years as an independent music teacher in Edina. She was the co-founder and chairman of the Applied Music Program in the Edina Public Schools. She was president of the Minneapolis Music Teachers Forum, the initial administrator for the MMTA syllabus program, and historian for MMTA.

7. The staff even took time during its Christmas/New Year break to consult. While the University of Manitoba caused this system to function, the private teachers of the area were quite opposed to the system because they had little input.

8. *Adventures* included small compositions by internationally known composers such as Toch, Kabalevsky, Bartók plus a good sampling of music by Minnesotans: Lynn Freeman Olson, Mary Davida Wood, Mary Margaret Mageau, Paul Fetler, Anne Riley, Eric Stokes, and Russell Harris. Rediger helped in the publication.

9. *MMTA Newsletter,* July 1973.

10. Ibid.

11. Bastien's work was published by Neil A Kjos in 1973. The quotation is on page 312.

12. Bastien, *How to Teach Piano,* pp. 322, 332–333. Besides relying on the printed materials, Bastien consulted Louise Guhl and Ethel Hascall of MMTA.

13. *MMTA Newsletter,* April, 1972. The state of Washington had a strong syllabus program and large student participation but seems to have been the only state beyond Minnesota so advanced.

14. Occasionally there were so many composition students worthy of recognition that a separate program had to be given.

15. *MMTA Newsletter,* November 1972, Report of Louise Guhl after a meeting with the Department.

16. Donald Ferguson, "The Piano Teacher and the Musical Public," *Proceedings of the Tenth Annual Convention of the Minnesota State Music Teachers' Association* (1911), p. 43.

17. *MMTA Newsletter,* February, 1973.

18. See Raymond Bechtle, "Private Music Lessons: A School Learning Opportunity," *The American Music Teacher,* April/May 1975, pp. 12–14, and Hascall's article in the *Newsletter,* October 1985. Just over a decade after this outcome, Russell Harris, long-time member and advocate, thought that across-the-board recognition should be still forthcoming although the members might feel like singing, "Lord, Lord how long!"

19. Mary Davida Wood, CSJ, (1911–1999), president of MMTA 1973–75, member of MMTA since 1932–1933, played piano commercially at an early age. She graduated in music from St. Catherine's College (1933), earned a Master's Degree from Columbia University (1941), and did advanced work at the Juilliard School, Pius X School of Liturgical Music, and Oxford University among many others. She taught a wide variety of musical subjects at St. Catherine's, 1932–1982, wrote many compositions and arrangements, served widely as a judge. She was a member of Delta Kappa Gamma, International Honor Society for Women in Education, and held many positions in the Zonta Club, International Service Organization for Executive Women.

20. *MMTA Newsletter,* August 1975.

21. Marguerite Hoffman, pianist, president of MMTA 1975-1977, studied at the School of Musical Art in Rochester, Minnesota, and with James Bonn and Sister Mary Davida Wood in St. Paul. Hoffman received the Artist Diploma from the American College of Musicians in Austin, Texas. She founded the Hoffman Music Studios, the Rochester Area Keyboard Club, and the Hiawathaland Festival, a competition for pianists in Rochester. She was responsible for organizing a central office for MMTA.

22. This account can only cover one small facet of music reading. More information can be found in the Sightplaying books of MMTA. The interested reader might also want read in Louise Guhl's *Odyssey of a Small Town Piano Teacher* the story of how she coped with reading problems and how she gradually arrived at her teaching series, *The Magic Reader.*

23. Gordon Howell of Canada, pianist, president of MMTA 1977–1979, studied first through the Royal Conservatory and McGill University. He earned the B.Mus. and M.Mus. degrees in piano from the MacPhail College in Minneapolis (1952–1954). He completed the Ph.D. at the Eastman School of Music in 1959 and from that date to his retirement in 1994 was chair of the Piano and Music Theory Divisions of Bethel College, St. Paul, Minnesota.

Chapter 11
A Work in Progress

1. John S. Adams and Barbara J. VanDrasek, *Minneapolis-St. Paul, People, Place, and Public Life,*(Minneapolis: University of Minnesota Press, 1993), p. 104.

2. Adams and VanDrasek, *Minneapolis-St. Paul,* p. 147.

3. See Frank M. Whiting, *Minnesota Theatre, From Old Fort Snelling to the Guthrie,* (Minneapolis: Pogo Press, 1988).

4. Kathleen T. Younker has written the development of this group as "The Central Minnesota Music Teachers Association, A Brief History" as a course paper at St. Cloud State University.

5. Report of the President in the *Newsletter* for July 1985.

6. *Report of the President, 1999.*

7. Waldo Selden Pratt writing in the American Supplement (1920) to the *Grove's Dictionary of Music and Musicians,* p. 302, noted even at that time that MTNA "has been cordial in relation to many other associations, even when they tended to deplete its own ranks."

8. The MTNA syllabus for high school auditions stated at the outset, "The National Audition can only represent the peak of a pyramiding national plan," the result of strong state and divisional auditions, *High School Student Activities-Auditions* (Cincinnati: NMTA, 1968–1969), p. 1.

9. Louise Guhl had special interest in this important topic and advised all committees. In 1976, she and Gwen Perun produced a video course, "Keyboard Sightreading," at the University of Minnesota. This topic continued to intrigue Guhl and eventually resulted in her study books, *The Magic Readers* published by Kjos.

10. The preface to the *Workbooks* lists the contributors from 1970 to 1995.

11. These patterns did not require any difficult fingering.

12. Steps beyond these basics came easily. It required only a change of one note to change from major mode to minor mode. Since there were only twelve basic patterns, the student could gradually learn to play the same small melody on each of these twelve notes, a process called transposition, something often thought to be a very advanced technique but here introduced as a normal process. Even the notation of intervals, steps of seconds written as line to space or space to line, or thirds as line to line or space to space, gave the student the look and feel of the music progressing, not something to be deciphered.

13. The two highest levels of the music theory program are designed for those special students with unusually great interest in the topic. For the piano examinations only the first four levels are required for the highest level in the piano syllabus. Because the demands on students' time are so pressing today, MMTA has now allowed students to take parts of the syllabus examination at various times during one year's time. Thus, a student might take the performance component, then the sight reading one and finally the music theory one.

14. This had been done in recognition of the difficulty of obtaining musical education in an earlier age.

15. E-mail from Sharon Kaplan. Kathryn Williamson and Mary Lou Iverson also contributed information on this topic.

16. *MMTA Newsletter,* September 1976.

17. See Seth Beckman and Jeffrey Graves, "Promoting Thoughtful Musical Collaboration," *American Music Teacher,* February/March 1997, pp. 20–24.

Chronology

1882   MINNESOTA'S FIRST DELEGATE TO MTNA
        William H. Leib becomes Vice-President for Minnesota

1887   FOUNDING OF THE FIRST MMTA, 19 October
        St. Paul: Ford's Music Hall
        President: Willard Patton

1892   MTNA CONVENTION planned for Minneapolis
        Cancelled, Demise of the first MMTA
        Some members continue to attend MTNA conventions

1901   MMTA ESTABLISHED, 27 June
        St. Paul: Raudenbush Hall
        MMTA's first constitution and officers
        President: Clarance Marshall
        The Professional League hosts the founding members

1902   CONVENTION, 19–20 May,
        St. Paul: Central Presbyterian Church
        President: Clarance Marshall
        Artist: Kneisel String Quartet,
        Minnesota Composers

1903   CONVENTION, 7–9 May
        Minneapolis: Plymouth & Wesley Churches
        President: Clarance Marshall
        Artists: Boston Festival Orchestra with Myrtle Weed, pianist
        Minnesota Composers

1904   CONVENTION, 16–18 June
        Duluth: First M. E. Church
        President: Eugene Murdock
        Artists: Emile Sauret, violinist; Arthur Speed, Pianist
        Minnesota Composers

1905   CONVENTION, 7–9 June
        Winona: First Congregational Church
        President: David Colville
        Artists: Mme. Hildegarde Hoffmann Huss, Soprano,
        Henry Holden Huss, American composer and pianist
        Minnesota Composers

1906   CONVENTION, 7–9 June
        Minneapolis: Plymouth Church
        President: Gustavus Johnson
        Artists: Charles Clark, baritone, Mary Angell, pianist
        Minnesota Composers

1907   CONVENTION, 6–8 June
        St. Paul: Central Presbyterian Church
        President: Clarance Marshall
        Artist: Emil Liebling, pianist
        Minnesota Composers

1908   CONVENTION, 16–18 June
        St. Peter: Gustavus Adolphus College
        President: Carlyle Scott
        Artist: Ernest R. Kroeger, organist and composer
        Minnesota Composers

1909   CONVENTION, 15–17 June
        Mankato: Presbyterian Church
        President: George Fairclough
        Artist: Henriot Levy, pianist

1910   CONVENTION, 21–23 June
        Detroit [Lakes]: Auditorium
        President: Willard Patton
        Artists from Minnesota
        Minnesota Composers

1911   CONVENTION, 9–11 May
        Minneapolis: Radisson Hotel
        President: Hamlin Hunt
        Artists from Minnesota
        Minnesota Composers

1912   CONVENTION, 4–6 June
        St. Paul: Ryan Hotel
        President: George A. Thornton
        Artists: Apollo Club (Minneapolis)
        Minnesota Composers

1912   CERTIFICATION PLAN APPROVED, 6 June
        Culmination of three years of discussion
        Based on the examples of organist's organizations
        3 levels: Fellow, Associate and Licentiate certificates

1913   FIRST TEST FOR LICENTIATE CERTIFICATE, 5 July
        Minneapolis, St. Paul, Duluth, Winona

1913   CONVENTION, 9–11 July
         Duluth: Spalding Hotel
         President: Heinrich Hoevel
         Artists from Duluth

1913   ARTICLES OF INCORPORATION, 20 October
         Minnesota Music, first issue, November

1914   CONVENTION, 23–25 June
         Minneapolis: West Hotel
         President: Leopold Bruenner
         Artists: MacPhail String Quartet
         Minnesota Composers

1915   CONVENTION, 22–24 June
         Albert Lea: Albert Lea College
         President: William MacPhail
         Artist: Mrs. Edward MacDowell, pianist-lecturer

1916   CONVENTION, 27–29 June
         Owatanna: Pillsbury Academy
         President: Harry Phillips
         Artists: Westminster Church Choir (Minneapolis)
            Bach Cantata "God's Time is Best"
         Florence Macbeth, contralto (Chicago Grand Opera)
         Program of "Modern Music"

1917   CONVENTION, 19–21 June
         Winona: College of St. Theresa
         President: J. Austin Williams
         Artist: Christine Miller, mezzo soprano

1918   CONVENTION, 25–27 June
         St. Paul: Hotel St. Paul
         President: Hamlin Hunt
         Artists: Westminster Church Choir (Brahms Requiem)
         Operetta by Stanley Avery "Cupid's Night Out"
         Frances Ingram, contralto (Chicago Grand Opera)

1919   CONVENTION, 19–21 June
         Northfield: Carleton College
         President: George Fairclough
         Artists: Theodore Spiering, violinist
         Edwin Arthur Kraft, organist

1920   CONVENTION, 22–24 June
         Minneapolis: Unitarian Church
         President: James Lang
         Artists: Elk's Glee Club, Percy Grainger, pianist
         Minnesota Composers,
         Minneapolis High School Composers

1921   CONVENTION, 21–23 June
        Duluth: YMCA Assembly Hall
        President: Elsie Shawe
        Artists from Minnesota
        Songs by Duluth Composers

1922   CONVENTION, 22–23 June
        St. Paul: Palm Room, St. Paul Hotel
        President: Stanley Avery
        Artist: E. Robert Schmitz, pianist

1922   100% AFFILIATION WITH MTNA, 22 August

1923   CONVENTION, 21–23 June
        Minneapolis: University of Minnesota (new Music Building)
        President: R. Buchanan Morton
        Artists: Hugo Goodwin, organist, Yeatman
        Griffith, vocalist, Leopold Auer, violinist,
        Josef Lhevinne, pianist

1924   CONVENTION, 18–20 June
        St. Paul: St. Paul Hotel
        President, R. Buchanan Morton
        Artists: Jeanette Vreeland, soprano,
        Edwin Hughes, pianist

1925   CONVENTION, 24–26 June
        Minneapolis: University of Minnesota
        President: Donald Ferguson
        Artists: Edwin Hughes, pianist, Herbert
        Witherspoon, bass, Franz Kneisel, violinist,
        Glenn Woods, public school musician,
        Frederick Lamond, pianist

1926   CONVENTION, 15–17 June
        St. Paul: St. Paul Hotel
        President: Donald Ferguson
        Artists: John Garns, psychologist,
        Lee Pattison, pianist, Hans Letz,
        violinist, William Brady, vocal teacher,
        Hugo Goodwin, organist
        First history of MMTA by Jessica De Wolf

1927   CONVENTION, 9–11 June
        Minneapolis: Music Building, University of Minnesota
        President: Donald Ferguson
        Artists: Gabriel Fenyves, pianist,
        Agnes Rast Snyder, contralto,
        Dudley Buck, voice teacher

1927   MTNA CONVENTION, 28–30 December
        Minneapolis: Radisson Hotel
        Local contribution: Minneapolis Symphony,
            Verbrugghen String Quartet, St. Olaf Choir,
            Eunice Norton, pianist

1928   CONVENTION, 17–20 May
        Minneapolis: Hotel Radisson
        President: J. Victor Bergquist
        Artists: Hugo Goodwin, organist,
        Helena Morsztyn, pianist
        High School Composers

1929   CONVENTION, 27–28 May
        St. Paul: Hotel Lowry
        President: J. Victor Bergquist
        Artists: Clara Stocker, composer,
        Alice Hokanson, organist

1930   CONVENTION, 17–18 June
        Minneapolis: Hotel Radisson
        President: Carl A. Jensen
        Special talk on Modernism, Dr. John Becker, composer
        Performance of an opera, "The Operatician"
        by Stanley Avery

1931   CONVENTION, 28–29 October
        St. Paul: Lowry Hotel
        Special talk on Pseudo Culture, Dr. John Becker, composer
        Performance of a Two-Act comic opera, "Captain Crossbones"
        by Arthur Penn

1932   CONVENTION, 26–27 October
        Minneapolis: Business Women's Club
        President: Harry W. Ranks
        Chamber music, a string quartet by Winnifred Reichmuth
        Concert by the Minneapolis Symphony

1933   CONVENTION, 24–25 October
        St. Paul: St. Paul Hotel
        President: Harry W. Ranks
        "A Century of Progress in American Music," (songs, dances)
        Selections from Bach's B-minor Mass
            by the Bach Society of the University of Minnesota,
        Artist: Lecture-Recital "The Young Pianist's Approach to
            Interpretation" by Dr. John Thompson

1934   CONVENTION, 30–31 October
        Minneapolis: Leamington Hotel
        President: Harry W. Ranks
        Johann Sebastian Bach Program by
            Rupert Sircom, organist and the Bach Society
            of the University of Minnesota
        Artist: Alfred Mirovitch, pianist

1935   CONVENTION, 28–30 October
        St. Paul: Lowry Hotel
        President: Harriet Allen (later Wilma Gilman)
        Bach Society of the University of Minnesota
        J. Victor Bergquist Memorial Concert
        Songs by the St. Paul Civic Opera Association
        Carleton College Symphony Band

1936   CONVENTION, 5 May
        St. Cloud: State Teachers' College
        President: Wilma Gilman
        "Music and the State" Dr. John Becker, composer
            and music director of the WPA
        Student composition: T. P. Giddings and Harry W. Ranks

1936   CONVENTION, 29–30 December
        Minneapolis: Nicollet Hotel
        President: Wilma Gilman
        Music in Japan
        Tributes to Hugo Goodwin and Heinrich Hoevel (deceased)

1936   FIRST CONCERT OF TEN MASSED PIANOS,
        30 December
            Becomes an annual event
        Minneapolis: Lyceum Theater
        Conducted by Percy Grainger

1937   CONVENTION, 18 June
        Alexandria
        President: Wilma Gilman
        Piano Clinic
        Minnesota Women Composers,
            Winnifred Reichmuth-Bolle, MarionAustin-Dunn,
            Helen A. Greim (& Robert Sheldon)

1937   CONVENTION, 22–23 November
        St. Paul: St. Paul Hotel
        President: Wilma Gilman
        Program by Winnipeg Artists
        Honored Guest, Minnie Boyd, President of Canadian
            Federation of Music Teachers' Associations
        Artist: Arthur Poister, organist

1938   CONVENTION, 21–22 November
         Minneapolis: Nicollet Hotel
         President: Chester Campbell
         Program by Cecil Burleigh, violinist & composer
         High School Composers

1939   CONVENTION, 29–31 October
         St. Paul: St. Paul Hotel
         President: Agnes Rast Snyder
         Artists: Frank Mannheimer, pianist,
         John Finley Williamson, choral conductor,
         Kurt Herbert Adler, conductor and accompanist

1940   CONVENTION, 26–27 June
         Duluth: Spalding Hotel
         President: Agnes Rast Snyder
         Artists: Frank Mannheimer, pianist, Walter
         Pfitzner, pianist, Nordic Choir, Peter Tkach, choral director

1940   CONVENTION, 10–12 November
         Minneapolis: Radisson Hotel
         President: Agnes Rast Snyder
         Artists: Rudolph Reutter, pianist, Dom
         Anselm Hughes, conductor & historian

1941   CONVENTION, 26–28 October
         St. Paul: Lowry Hotel
         President: Agnes Rast Snyder
         Artists: Julian DeGray, pianist, Jenny Cullen, violinist
         Minnesota Women Composers
             Helen A. Greim, Virginia W. Powell, Nina Marie St. John,
             (& Walther Pfitzner)

1941   MTNA CONVENTION, 26–31 December
         Minneapolis: Hotel Nicollet
         National President: Glen Haydon
         Minnesota Vice-President of MTNA: Carlyle Scott
         Contemporary American Piano Music: John Kirkpatrick
         Cello & Piano: Nikolai & Joanna Graudan
         WPA & University Symphonies: Abe Pepinsky
         American Music: Minneapolis Symphony & Howard Hanson
         Songs by Russell Harris
         Catholic Choral Society of St. Paul: Father Missia
         Hamline University Choir: John Kuypers
         Apollo Club: William MacPhail
         West High School a Cappella Choir: Peter Tkach

1942   CONVENTION, 1–2 November
        Minneapolis: Nicollet Hotel
        President: Agnes Rast Snyder
        Organ and Choral Concert (Roosevelt HS Chorus,
            Rupert Sircom, organist, & Basilica Choir)
        Artist: Hazel Griggs, pianist

1943   CONVENTION, 31 October–1 November
        Saint Paul: Lowry Hotel
        President: Agnes Rast Snyder
        "Panorama of American History" by the
            speech fraternity Zeta Phi Eta
        Harrison Wall Johnson, pianist
        Johnson High School Chorus

1944   CONVENTION, 29–30 October
        Minneapolis: University of Minnesota
        President: Agnes Rast Snyder
        "A Salute to the Nations of the World" by the
            speech fraternity Zeta Phi Eta
        Artists: Minneapolis String Quartet

1945   CONVENTION, 28–29 October
        Minneapolis: University of Minnesota
        President: Carl A. Jensen
        Gregorian Chant Rehearsal (Father Keller, OSB)
        Harding HS Madrigal Singers
        High School Composers
        Artists: Louis Crowder, pianist, Louis Krasner,
            violinist with Ernst Krenek, pianist

1946   CONVENTION, 23–24 June
        Minneapolis: University of Minnesota
        President: Carl A. Jensen
        Artists: Julian DeGray, pianist, Arthur Jennings, organist

1947   CONVENTION, 16–17 June
        Minneapolis: University of Minnesota
        President: Carl A. Jensen
        The Church Music Institute
        Artist: Gunnar Johansen, pianist

1948   CONVENTION, 14–15 June
        Minneapolis: Scott Hall (formerly the Music Building)
            (now named to honor Mr. and Mrs. Carlyle Scott)
        President: Robert N. Pearson
        Artists: Felix Witzinger, pianist, Elie Siegmeister, composer
            & folklorist

1949   CONVENTION, 19–20 June
Minneapolis: Scott Hall
President: Paul M. Oberg
State Honors Student Concert, Northrop Auditorium
*From this point on, the massed piano event was held at
Northrop Auditorium of the University of Minnesota the
evening before the main convention*
Artists: Rudolph Ganz, pianist, Martial Singher, baritone

1950   CONVENTION, 18–19 June
Minneapolis: Scott Hall
President: Paul M. Oberg
Artists: Julian DeGray, pianist, Désiré Ligeti, bass-baritone,
June Weybright, composer-piano teacher

1951   CONVENTION, 17–18 June
Minneapolis: Scott Hall
President: Paul M. Oberg
Artist: Maurice Dumesnil, pianist

1952   CONVENTION, 15–17 June
Minneapolis: Scott Hall
President: Paul M. Oberg
Artist: Frank Glazer, pianist

1953   CONVENTION, 14–15 June
Minneapolis: Scott Hall
President: Dora Gosso
Artists: Monte Hill Davis, pianist,
Silvio Scionti, pianist-teacher-jurist

1954   CONVENTION, 13–14 June
Minneapolis: Scott Hall
President: Dora Gosso
Artist: Bernhard Weiser, pianist

1955   CONVENTION, 19–20 June
Minneapolis: Scott Hall
President: Dora Gosso
Artist: Thaddeus Kozuch, pianist

1956   CONVENTION, 17–18 June
Minneapolis: Scott Hall
President: Russell G. Harris
Artists: Rupert Sircom, organist, Roy Schuesler,
baritone, Thelma Hunter, pianist, Robert Andersen
String Ensemble

1957   CONVENTION, 23–24 June
Minneapolis: Scott Hall
President: Anthony Chiuminatto
Artists: Bernhard Weiser, pianist, Aksel Schiotz, baritone,
Trio da Camera, Messiah Lutheran Choir

1958   First *MMTA Newsletter*, January

1958   MTNA EAST CENTRAL DIVISION CONVENTION,
        16–19 Feb.
(with the American String Teachers National Convention)
Minneapolis: Pick-Nicollet Hotel
President: Russell Harris
Minnesota Artists: Marjorie Briggs & Thelma Hunter, duo-
pianists, Augsburg College Choir, Paul Manz, organist,
St. Olaf College Vocal Ensemble, Shirley Kartarik, soprano,
University of Minnesota Opera Workshop, Chamber Singers
and Chorus, Adyline Johnson, contralto

1958   CONVENTION, 22–23 June
Minneapolis: Scott Hall
President: Anthony Chiuminatto
Nicholas Slonimsky lecture on modern music
Artists: Anton Kuerti, pianist, Marjorie McClung, soprano

1959   CONVENTION, 21–23 June
Minneapolis: Scott Hall
President: John Thut
Artists: Norman Abelson, bass-baritone, Rosen
String Quartet, John Simms, pianist

1960   CONVENTION, 12–14 June
Minneapolis: Scott Hall
President: John Thut
Artists: Gunnar Johansen, pianist, Anna Kaskas, vocal
teacher, University of Minnesota Opera Workshop

1961   CONVENTION, 11–13 June
Minneapolis: Scott Hall
President: John Thut
3-tiered certification approved
Artists: John Simms, pianist, Dallas Draper, tenor.
Norman Carol, violinist, Eva Knardahl, pianist, Paul
Freed, pianist

1962   CONVENTION, 10–12 June
Minneapolis: Coffman Memorial Union
President: Robert Laudon
MMTA office established at State Organization Services
Group medical insurance plan approved (started by Thut)
University of North Dakota Trio

1963   CONVENTION, 16–17 June
            Minneapolis: Coffman Memorial Union
            President: Robert Laudon
            Artists: Storm Bull, pianist, Leslie Chabay, tenor

1964   CONVENTION, 14–15 June
            Minneapolis: Coffman Memorial Union
            President: Roy Schuessler
            New Theory Tests featured
            Artists: Heinrich Fleischer, organist, Donald Betts,
            pianist, Sr. Macrina Manderfeld, flautist, Sr. Mary Helene
            Juettner, soprano, Sr. Ellen Cotone, pianist

1965   TRIAL THEORY TESTS offered for first time, May

1965   CONVENTION, 13–14 June
            Minneapolis: Coffman Memorial Union
            President: Roy Schuessler
            Contemporary Music
            Artist: Bernhard Weiser, pianist

1966   CONVENTION, 12–13 June
            Minneapolis: Coffman Memorial Union
            President: Anthony Chiuminatto
            Artists: Flor String Quartet

1967   CONVENTION, 11–12 June
            Minneapolis: Coffman Memorial Union
            President: Anthony Chiuminatto
            First MTNA certification plan annouced
            Artists: MMTA members
            Young Artist Program

1967   First membership directory

1968   CONVENTION, 9–10 June
            St. Paul: Janet Wallace Center, Macalester College
            President: Paul W. Freed
            New constitution & 3-phase development plan approved
            Young Artist Program

1969   CONVENTION, 8–9 June
            St. Paul: Janet Wallace Center, Macalester College
            President: Paul W. Freed
            Royal Conservatory of Toronto Syllabus, Margaret Poole,
            Young Artists Program

1969   GRANT from Bremer Foundation, $2,500, December
            For publication of syllabus

1970   MTNA WEST CENTRAL DIVISION CONFERENCE,
            25–27 Jan.
        Minneapolis: Hotel Leamington
        Local Chairman: Paul W. Freed

1970   GRANT from Bush Foundation, $12,350, May
        For research and development of the syllabus

1970   CONVENTION, 14–16 June
        St. Paul: Janet Wallace Center, Macalester College
        President: Shirley Rediger
        The Syllabus Project
        Artist: John Perry, pianist

1970   PIANO THEORY Examination Syllabus published, Oct.

1971   CONVENTION, 13–15 June
        St. Paul: Janet Wallace Center, Macalester College
        President: Shirley Rediger
        First awards to student composition winners
        Artists: Howard Karp, pianist, True Sackrison, cellist
        & Robert Whitcomb, pianist-composer, Margaret Gignac-
        Hedges, soprano,
        Young Artist Program

1972   CONVENTION, 18–19 June
        St. Paul: Janet Wallace Center, Macalester College
        President: Louise Guhl
        Revision of Constitution and Certification plan
        Certification renewal required every 5 years
        Artist: Bernhard Weiser, pianist

1973   CONVENTION, 10–11 June
        St. Paul: Music Building, College of Saint Catherine
        President: Louise Guhl
        Young Artist and Composer Recital
            *From this point onward, each convention had a special
            program featuring the prize-winning performers and stu-
            dent composers.*
        Artist: Irene A. Glasford, pianist-teacher

1973   PUBLICATION of Vol. 1 of *Adventures in Time and Space*

1974   CONVENTION, 9–10 June
        St. Paul: Music Building, College of Saint Catherine
        President: Mary Davida Wood, CSJ
        Edina Plan of applied instruction for credit discussed
        Artists: Allison Nelson, pianist, Robert Scoggin,
        organist, Patricia Scoggin, cellist

1975   CONVENTION, 8–10 June
        St. Paul: Prom Center
        President: Mary Davida Wood, CSJ
        Committee appointed on Sight Reading and Accompaniment
        Artist: Thomas Richner, pianist, lecturer on Mozart

1976   CONVENTION, 13–15 June
        St. Paul: Prom Center
        President: Marguerite Hoffman
        Central Office replaced State Organization Services
        Artist: Eduardo Delgado, pianist, lecture/recital of music
            of Argentina

1977   CONVENTION, 12–14 June
        St. Paul: Prom Center
        President: Marguerite Hoffman
        Artists: Dallas Weekley & Nancy Arganbright, duo-pianists,
        Sheryl Woods, coloratura soprano, Arthur F. Becknell,
        accompanist and eurythmics

1978   CONVENTION, 11–13 June
        St. Paul: Prom Center
        President: Gordon Howell
        Piano Syllabus Revision
        Artists: Paul Pollei, pianist, Carol Nelson,
        child psychologist, Mark Bjork, Suzuki teacher of violin

1978   First of annual MMTA Calendars mailed, October

1979   CONVENTION, 17–19 June
        St. Paul: Prom Center
        President: Gordon Howell
        Artist: Arthur Tollefson, pianist

1980   CONVENTION, 7–9 June
        St. Paul: O'Shaughnessy Education Center
        (College of St. Thomas)
        President: Phyllis Peabody
        Artists: Nelita True, pianist, Martha Hilley,
        class piano

1981   CONVENTION, 6–8 June
        St. Paul: O'Shaughnessy Education Center
        President: Phyllis Peabody
        Celebration of MMTA's 80th Anniversary
        Piano Syllabus Revision
        Guest, Henry Steinway
        Artist: Mary Ann Covert, pianist

1982   CONVENTION, 5–7 June
        St. Paul: O'Schaughnessy Education Center
        President: Jean Hegland
        Commissioned composition premiered:
            Dragons for piano four-hands by Carol Barnett
        Artist: Eiji Hashimoto, harpsichordist

1983   CONVENTION, 4–6 June
        St. Paul: O'Schaughnessy Education Center
        President: Jean Hegland
        Song Recital in memory of Roy Schuessler
        Commissioned composition premiered:
            Chi by Janika Vandevelde
        Music and the Microcomputer
        Artists: Samuel Sanders, accompanist,
        Judy Schubert, soprano and Christine Dahl, pianist

1984   CONVENTION, 2–4 June
        St. Paul: O'Schaughnessy Education Center
        President: Russell G. Harris
        First convention with overlapping sessions for various topics
            From this point onward, convention schedules had 2–3
            events for each time slot enabling those attending to choose
            subjects of particular interest and also enabling MMTA *to*
            feature members with special expertise as presenters
        Minnesota Winners MTNA Auditions
        Artist: Veda Zuponic, pianist

1984   Duet Composition Contest for MMTA members
        becomes annual event

1985   CONVENTION, 1–3 June
        St. Paul: O'Schaughnessy Education Center
        President: Russell G. Harris
        Report on Violin Syllabus & Voice Syllabus testing
        Artist: Robert Shannon, pianist

1986   CONVENTION, 7–10 June
        St. Paul: O'Schaughnessy Education Center
        President: Marian M. Hutt
        Artists: Tony Caramia, jazz pianist,
        Mary Almjeld Veverka, pianist

1987   CONVENTION, 6–9 June
        Roseville: Northwestern College
        President: Marian M. Hutt
        Artist: Frank H. Wiens, pianist

1987   FIRST EUROPEAN STUDY TOUR, Central Europe,
24 July–13 August
*These tours are planned with a knowledgable leader who
gave lectures and musical illustrations (even on bus rides).
College credit or credit toward MMTA certification is
given for successful completion of the tour and study sessions preceding.*

1987   FIRST ENSEMBLE FESTIVAL, *continued annually*

1988   CONVENTION, 4–7 June
Roseville: Northwestern College
President: Ruth V. Anderson
Artists: Phyllis Alpert Lehrer, pianist, Linda Hirt,
pianist, Philip Kraus, baritone

1989   CONVENTION, 4–6 June
Roseville: Northwestern College
President: Ruth V. Anderson
First comprehensive convention booklet with reports
    continued annually
Piano Syllabus Revision
Artists: Alan & Alvin Chow, duo-pianists,
Roger Martin, flute & Kathleen Rountree, piano

1989   European study tour, Italy, 15 June–2 July

1990   CONVENTION, 3–5 1990
Roseville: Northwestern College
President: Mary Ann Hanley, CSJ
Theme: A Global Perspective
    First convention organized around a theme
Artists: Minnesota Musicians

1991   CONVENTION, 2–4 June
Roseville: Northwestern College
President: Mary Ann Hanley, CSJ
Celebration of MMTA's 90th Anniversary
Theme: Mozart and the Classical Period
Opera: *Mozart and Salieri* by Rimski-Korsakov
Piano Portrait: Mozart
Artists: John Kenneth Adams, pianist, Alan Bryan, bass,
Rick Penning, tenor

1991   European study tour, France, 4–24 July

1992   CONVENTION, 7–9 June
Roseville: Northwestern College
President: Kay M. Koehnen
Theme: A Focus on American Music
Artists: John Salmon, jazz & classical pianist,
Michael Scott, arranger and composer

1993   CONVENTION, 6–8 June
        Roseville: Northwestern College
        President: Kay M. Koehnen
        Theme: Practical Approaches to Creative Teaching
        Session on computers for Business and Theory
        Artist: Robert Weirich, pianist

1993   European study tour, England, Wales & Scotland
            7–24 July

1994   CONVENTION, 5–7 June
        Roseville: Northwestern College
        President: Raeanna Gislason
        Theme: Romantic Energy
        All-Chopin Recital
        Artist: Rebecca Penneys, pianist

1995   CONVENTION, 5–6 June
        Roseville: Northwestern College
        President: Raeanna Gislason
        Theme: Musical Imagery
        Session on Electronic Keyboards
        Clinician, Maurice Hinson, pianist-researcher
        Artist: Paul Shaw

1995   European study tour, Spain & Portugal,
            27 July–15 August

1995   FIRST EDUCATIONAL FORUM, 22 August
        Collegeville, St. John's University
        "Variations on a Classical Theme"

1996   CONVENTION, 3–4 June
        Roseville: Northwestern College
        President: Mary A. Brandenburg
        Theme: Bach to Jazz
        Clinician: Julie Jaffee Nagel
        Artists: Louis Nagel, pianist, Julia & Irina Elkina,
        duo-pianists

1996   SECOND EDUCATION FORUM 13 August
        Collegeville: St. John's University
        "Baroque Treasures"

1997   CONVENTION, 2–3 June
        Roseville: Northwestern College
        President: Mary A. Brandenburg
        Theme: Young Artists
        Artists: Dallas Weekley & Nancy Arganbright, duo-pianists,
        Butch Thompson, jazz pianist

1997   European study tour, Scandinavia, 24 June–13 July

1997   THIRD EDUCATIONAL FORUM, 19 August
        Collegeville, St. John's University
        "Contemporary Pleasures"

1998   CONVENTION, 1–2 June
        St. Paul: Historic St. Paul Hotel
        President: Kathleen H. Hasse
        Theme: Music in an International Rose Garden
        Artists: Paul Shaw, pianist, Paul Wirth, pianist

1998   FOURTH EDUCATIONAL FORUM, 18 August
        Collegeville: St. John's University
        "Romantic Measures"

1999   CONVENTION, 7–8 June
        Brooklyn Park: Northwest Inn & Conference Center
        President: Kathleen H. Hasse
        Theme: The Gift of Music
        Artist: John Perry, pianist

1999   European study tour, Belgium & Netherlands,
            15 July–4 August

Photo Credits

53 Minneapolis Public Library, Minneapolis Collection

67 Rank, Minneapolis Public Library, Minneapolis Collection

67 Jensen, Macalester College Archives

70 Early MMTA Archives, Minnesota Historical Society

71 Minnesota Historical Society

73 Charcoal Sketch by Robert Koehler, original not located, from a newspaper clipping courtesy of Frances Miller Aspnes (Wilma Anderson's daughter)

74 Early MMTA Archives, Minnesota Historical Society

77 Minneapolis Public Library, Minneapolis Collection

78 University of Minnesota Archives

81 Minnesota Historical Society

82 Minnesota Historical Society

84 Augsburg College Archives

88 MMTA Historian's File

89 The Markley Family

90 Brunelle, *St. Paul Dispatch & Pioneer Press*, 17 June 1979

90 Concert, *St. Paul Dispatch & Pioneer Press*, 17 June 1979

95 *St. Paul Dispatch & Pioneer Press*, 20 Feb. 1971

96 University of Minnesota School of Music

98 St. Thomas College Archives

106 Neil A. Kjos Music Company

114 Mitchell Photography (Edina, MN)

121 Raeanna Gislason

129 Katherine R. Bina

132 *Fourth Annual Catalogue of the Johnson School* (1901–1902), Minnesota Historical Society

133 Florence A. Blattner

134 In Portugal, Marion Hutt

134 On the bus, Jan Bruder

134 In Edinburgh, Hyldred Peterson

136 Krinke, Larry Marcus Photography (Minneapolis)

136 Graves, Raeanna Gislason

Other photos contributed by the subjects

Index

number in *italics* indicates an illustration

bio indicates biography